CEDAR MILL COMMUNITY LIBRARY
12505 NW CORNELL RD
PORTLAND, OR 97229
(503-644-0043)
WASHINGTON COUNTY COOPERATIVE
WITHDRAWN LIBRARY SERVICES
CEDAR MILL LIBRARY

GOLD PANNER'S MANUAL

GARNET BASQUE

The Lyons Press

COPYRIGHT © 1974, 1991 GARNET BASQUE

LIBRARY OF CONGRESS CATALOGING-IN-PUBLICATION DATA

Basque, Garnet.
    Gold panner's manual / Garnet Basque.
        p.   cm.
    Originally published: Langley, B.C. : Stagecoach Pub. Co., 1974.
    Includes bibliographical references.
    ISBN 1-55821-873-4
    1. Gold mines and mining—Handbooks, manuals, etc.
    2. Hydraulic mining—Handbooks, manuals, etc. I. Title.

    TN421.B38 1999   98-45011
        622'.3422—dc21   CIP

PRINTING HISTORY
Published July 1974, reprinted 1975.
Revised second edition, May 1976, reprinted 1977, 1978, 1979, 1980.
Revised third edition, May 1983, reprinted 1985, 1988.
Revised fourth edition, October 1991, reprinted 1996, 1999.
First Lyons Press edition, 1999.

10 9 8 7 6 5 4 3 2 1

ALL RIGHTS RESERVED. No part of this publication may be
reproduced, stored in a retrieval system, or transmitted in any form or
by any means—electronic, mechanical, photocopying, audio recording,
or otherwise—without the written consent of the publisher. All
inquiries should be addressed to: The Lyons Press, 123 West 18 Street,
New York, New York 10011.

THE LYONS PRESS
123 West 18 Street, New York, New York 10011

Printed in Hong Kong

Contents

Introduction

GOLD! Of all the words in the English language, surely this must be the most magic of all — GOLD!

From time unknown, man has cherished and saved, laboured for, murdered for, waged wars for, and altered the course of history, in his quest for this elusive yellow metal.

Today, after almost 40 years of having been pegged by the United States government at the "artificial" value of $35 an ounce, gold is once again a free commodity on the world market and has soared to more than $850 an ounce. At the time of writing, gold is currently fluctuating in the $440-$460 an ounce range, with many analysts predicting that a price of $2,000 an ounce is not out of the question in the next few years.

Now, for the first time in a century, long-abandoned mining claims have been re-staked and reworked, and thousands of weekend prospectors, and professionals, for that matter, are loading their gold pans and camping gear into the family wagon for a Saturday-Sunday excursion along the creek beds where, 100 and more years ago, prospectors picked and panned their way to a fortune.

Countless others are doing their own "thing" in antique stores, searching for those golden family heirlooms and curios. For gold is where you find it, and be it in the form of an old pocket watch, or crude nugget, it can reap its owner a sizeable reward on today's market.

Recently, a newspaper article reported that, for the first time in 75 years, "gold fever is returning to Dawson City," home of the historic Klondike gold rush. Almost a century ago, the banks of the Yukon River yielded the richest treasure in modern history, creating the greatest gold rush the world has ever seen, before its glittering treasure was tapped.

But today, with gold at high levels, new interest is being shown in the historic riverbanks which, in 1897-98, drew tens of thousands of men and women from every walk of life, and every corner of the globe. Today, for the first time in nearly a century, every square foot of Bonanza and Eldorado creeks, site of the most feverish activity during the Klondike excitement, has again been staked and is being worked, by weekend amateur and large syndicate alike.

Yet others are doing their "mining" in the collection of coins, objects d'art, and bullion, in the belief that gold is the only sure hedge against worsening inflation. . . .

Whatever one's reason for becoming interested in gold — and who is not — in succeeding pages, author Garnet Basque has compiled a fascinating, factual and comprehensive history of gold, complete with details of how to search for — and how to find — nuggets and placer lodes; perhaps even the fabled "mother lode."

But there is no reward greater than that of fresh air and exercise and, if nothing else, amateur prospectors are sure to find plenty of both in the Canadian and American outdoors. For gold, as I mentioned, is where you find it. If nothing else, think of those golden memories!

Pleasant reading. . . .

T.W. Paterson

CHAPTER ONE

Gold Throughout The Ages

GOLD has been known and valued since prehistoric times. Because gold occurs freely in nature and has a distinctive appearance it is believed to have been one of the first metals discovered by ancient man.

In the misty remoteness of a thousand centuries ago, a scantily-clad caveman, scavenging for food, became the first human to set eyes upon the precious metal. Attracted by the bright glint of placer gold in an ancient stream bed, the Stone Age prospector noted its weight, admired its fine and lustrous colour, and possibly, polished it against his rough animal-like skin garments. As the centuries passed, man learned to mould the soft yellow metal into crude trinkets, then rough forms of jewellery, and eventually, into exquisite, finely-crafted gold-work.

However, it was not until about 6,000 years ago that gold became readily available to man. By the year 5000 BC, working with gold became a highly skilled art. Some Egyptian inscriptions showing gold being mined and refined were probably made before 4000 BC, and ancient gold mines discovered in Egypt are believed to be at least that old. Between 4000-3000 BC, Sumerian sun worshippers, who had created a disciplined religious organization in the southern part of ancient Mesopotamia, constructed towers sheathed in tons of gold. Beautifully crafted vessels of gold, dating from c3000-2340 BC, have been unearthed at Ur in Mesopotamia (now Iraq). These fine examples of Sumerian craftsmanship vividly prove their skill with gold, silver and copper.

By this time gold had become a highly prized commodity — and out of reach of the common man. It became a symbol of supreme power, being reserved for the priesthood and rulers. It was used in temples and the tombs of kings, to equip massive armies, and to reward successful conquerors.

The Egyptians were first to really exploit the larger known gold-mining regions of ancient times. One such area, Upper Egypt proper, consisted of a plateau some 60 miles wide and bordered the Red Sea for almost 200 miles, from Philoteras, to a point below Berenice. The second region, known in antiquity as Nubia, stretched east and west between the Nile River and the Red Sea.

Although the Egyptians were not the first to discover gold, they were the first people to undertake an active, intelligent and wide-ranging search for it. They were well organized and carefully controlled the production and use of the precious metal. They also amassed much gold through conquests. The Sumerians lost their gold to the conquering Egyptians, who desired it for their dying pharaohs so that they might appease their 2,000 gods and buy immortality for their souls.

The Egyptians created ornaments, vessels, idols, and jewellery with lavish decorations and great technical proficiency. Egyptian gold-work, dating from the Middle Kingdom, including gold jewellery with inlaid gems, and gold objects recovered from the tomb of King Tutankhamen, are examples of the exquisite work done by Egypt's goldsmiths. Tutankhamen's tomb, which was discovered intact in 1922, contained thousands of objects, including a gold, silver and jewelled thrown, and gilded chariots. The mummy was enclosed in three nested coffins, all splendidly ornamented, and the innermost one of gold. The coffin, weighing 224 pounds of beaten gold, decorated inside and out, was for many years on display in Cairo. However, since the 1967 Arab-Israeli war, it has been placed in a secret hiding place.

The Egyptians also knew how to hammer gold into leaves so thin, that over 250,000 such leaves, placed one atop the other, would make a pile only one inch thick!

King Menes, first historic ruler of the dynasty of ancient Egypt, had gold cast into small 14-gram bars with his name imprinted. As these bars were legal tender, they could actually be considered a form of ancient money. In China, where gold was scarce, cubes of gold were used as money as early as 2100 BC.

Unfortunately, of the 5,000,000 pounds of fine gold produced by the Egyptians, or taken in conquest, very little has survived in its original form. A few magnificent bracelets of the 31st century BC, an exquisite hawk's head of beaten gold from Hierakonpolis, the stunning personal jewels of Princess Khnumet and the undisturbed tomb of King Tutankhamen, are all that have survived to the present. The bracelets mentioned above came from the tomb of King Zer, and are the earliest examples of Egyptian jewellery in existence.

The vast majority of fine Egyptian gold-work had gone into their temples and elaborate tombs, and these locations were systematically looted by gangs or organized robbers. Tragically, these fabulous works of art were melted down into ingots, to eventually turn up in the form of gold coins.

The conquest for gold sent Roman legions to Britain, Portuguese sailors around Africa to the Orient, Columbus to the New World, forty-niners to California, and sourdoughs to Alaska and the Yukon.

Gold-work of the Aegean civilization, a Bronze Age culture that began on an island of Crete before 2500 BC, shows the many metal-working techniques — openwork, repousse, embossing, and inlaying — used by the craftsmen of that time. The Valphio Cups are the most outstanding treasures to have survived this period, although many fine examples of gold-work (jewellery, death masks, drinking cups, vases, weapons, and dress ornaments) have been found at Troy, Mycenae, and Tiryns.

Because of its key geographical position, at the very crossroads of maritime traffic in the Aegean Sea, the Island of Crete became the first nation in the eastern Mediterranean, other than Egypt, to come into possession of any notable quantities of gold. Crete obtained its gold through trade and in far-reaching travel, as natural gold was non-existent on the island itself.

The gold-work of the Archaemenid dynasty of Persia (600-800 BC), is noted for its extreme opulence and the technical skill with which it was executed.

Gold, as previously stated, was frequently used for equipping armies. The crafty Persians, however, used portions of their reserves to bribe one potential enemy into war against another potential enemy. After the battle, one enemy would invariably be destroyed, and the other would be so weakened by the conflict, that the Persians encountered little difficulty in reclaiming their gold, plus all the treasures accumulated by their enemies.

Archaic Greek and Etruscan gold-work dating from c700-500 BC was strongly influenced by Near Eastern designs. With its rich and barbaric imagery, Etruscan gold-work was among the finest in the ancient world. Later Greek work developed exquisite filigree and combined delicate geometric ornaments with mythological figures. Roman gold-work followed Greek forms, but placed greater emphasis on massive proportions and elaborate detail.

In ancient times, gold changed hands frequently, mostly as a result of bloody wars or conquests. The Roman Emperor Trajan captured 500,000 pounds of gold from the Dacians in the two wars of AD 102 and AD 105. Dacia (now Rumania) then became a Roman province.

Alexander the Great, one of the most powerful personalities of antiquity, and one of the greatest generals of all time, seized the royal treasure of Susa containing 2,000,000 pounds of gold and silver ingots, and 500,000 pounds of gold coins. It is said that an army of mules and camels was needed to carry the treasure to Babylon.

Alexander's wealth would probably have been the most bountiful in history, had he been able to capture the royal treasure of Darius III, the Persian king. Darius was defeated in the battle of Issus (333 BC) and again in the battle of Gaugamela, near Arbela (331 BC), after twice underestimating Alexander's strength. However, Darius succeeded in burying the royal treasure somewhere around Hamandan, midway between Bagdad and the Caspian Sea.

Although Alexander had the countryside torn asunder and ordered

This woodcut from **Da Natura Fossilium** *(1547), illustrates the method employed by the Romans in extracting gold. Lacking explosives, a fire was set against the rock face, and, when sufficiently heated, cold water was thrust upon it. This rapid change in temperature would shatter the rock. The smaller chunks were then hammered to free the gold.*

hundreds killed in his attempt to locate the Persian treasure — the production of several centuries — he found nothing. Future leaders, including Crassus, Marc Anthony, Augustus, Gaius, Germanicus and Nero, searched for the massive treasure. The occasional piece of jewellery, coins, and a few ingots were uncovered, but the bulk of the royal treasure remains hidden. The search continued into modern times in the same general area.

Egypt remained the richest gold-producing area in the world until the conquering Romans began exploiting Spanish deposits. By the 1st century AD, Roman control of Spain was virtually complete, and it was here that Roman engineers performed astounding feats of engineering skill in their quest for gold. They sank shafts deep within the earth, and washed down entire mountains; then directed water from heights of 400 to 800 feet against the collapsed mountain of debris to wash out the gold.

The Romans ventilated their mines by numerous adits, or passage-ways, which sloped down gradually from the surface. They employed waterwheels and other ingenious pumping devices to drain their mines, and although they had no explosives, they devised a method for breaking the hardest rock. This method, called fire setting, was accomplished when the rock was heated by a fire set against it. When sufficiently heated, cold water was thrust against the rock, creating a rapid change in temperature which would shatter it.

The gold was then shipped to Rome through the Port of Seville. Centuries after, when Spain became the conqueror of the New World, the gold flowed back into the royal Spanish coffers through this same port.

Unlike ancient Egypt, which had reserved its gold for its kings, the Romans accelerated the distribution of the precious yellow metal among private citizens. In Roman society it was possible for private citizens to amass individual fortunes in gold.

During the early Middle Ages, the best European gold-work was produced by the Celts, particularly in Ireland. When Rome conquered what is now England, she extracted enormous quantities of gold from the Celts.

Spain's golden wealth began to emerge when Francisco Pizarro, illiterate and hungry for gold, set sail for the New World. In 1532 Pizarro landed in Peru with less than 200 men. He was greeted by Atahualpa, the Inca chief and 10,000 unarmed men. As the Spaniards, pretending friendship, neared the chief, they attacked, instantly killing most of the native leaders, and holding Atahualpa for ransom. For his freedom, Atahualpa offered to fill the large room in which he was held prisoner with gold, and two smaller ones with silver. Pizarro agreed to these terms, amassing $100,000,000 in gold and silver, then treacherously had Atahualpa executed. In one of the worst cultural tragedies in history, the conquering Spaniards forced the Inca Indians to melt down their superb, beautiful gold-work — the results of 2,000 years of craftsmanship — into ingots. What little survived their murderous plunder was hidden, apparently for eternity, in the high mountains of the Andes. In the same year, Pizarro marched south, taking and looting the Inca capital of Cuzco.

Following the conquest of South America, the Spaniards focused their attention on Mexico and the southwestern United States, ranging as far north as California and Washington. Numerous claims were located and worked, usually through enslaved labour, and soon fleets of gold-laden ships were transporting the priceless cargo to Spain. During the War of Spanish Succession (1701-1713), much of the riches in coin and bullion was stored because of the lack of shipping. When the war ended, a fleet, accompanied by armed galleons, was dispatched to bring the wealth back to Spain. Estimates — based upon old records — are that some $15,000,000 in gold and silver was included in the fleet that set sail from Havana.

Five days out from the Cuban port, the flotilla was caught in a hurricane in the Bahama Channel. Ten of the 11 ships were sunk, with more than 1,000 crewmen and the entire treasure being lost.

An early engraving of Sutter's Mill, California, where gold was discovered by James Marshall in 1848.

Portugal was the next nation to accumulate large quantities of gold. In the 1780s, gold and diamonds were discovered in Brazil, and Portugal's prosperity, after a disastrous earthquake in 1755, was restored. In the 18th century alone, Portuguese treasure fleets transported 1,750,000 pounds of gold dust from Brazil. They also acquired large quantities of Japanese gold.

Except for the recoveries of gold by the Indians and the Spanish conquistadors, gold was first discovered and mined in the United States in North Carolina in 1799. But these deposits, although rich, were relatively small and quickly depleted. This initial discovery was followed by others in the 1820s and 1830s in several Appalachian states which produced significant amounts of gold prior to the American Civil War.

Then, on January 24, 1848, James W. Marshall, a carpenter building a sawmill in partnership with John A. Sutter, noticed flakes of yellow metal in the millrace of the American River, about 35 miles northeast of Sacramento. This initial discovery prompted examination of other California rivers that originated in the Sierras, and within a few months every stream along the western slope was being worked for gold. Sparked by these discoveries, the world's first gold rush focused

An early engraving of prospector's panning for gold.

attention upon California, as the news spread up and down the West Coast, to the eastern states, across the border to Mexico, and even to the Sandwich Islands (now Hawaii). Although thousands were killed by an epidemic of Asiatic cholera, California's population rose to more than 90,000 by the end of 1849 and soared to about 250,000 by 1852, the year in which gold production reached its peak. The influx of prospectors that reached California during the first few years of the rush indirectly led to the colonization of the entire western United States.

In the earliest days of the rush, claims yielding as much as $300 to $400 in a day were not uncommon, and in the first year about $10,000,000 in gold was mined.

One of the prospectors, E.H. Hargraves, who arrived in 1849, was amazed by the striking similarity between the geographical features of California and those of his native Australia. Rushing back to Australia, he discovered a vast field of both placer and lode deposits, and sparked the great Australian gold rush of 1851. Large quantities of gold were first discovered in the Bathurst district west of Sydney, and then in the hills around Melbourne. Within four years the flood of immigrants, from England alone, numbered 1,250,000. Other gold rushes occurred in Western Australia, beginning in 1892, when gold was discovered at Coolgardie and Kalooorie. The latter is still a profitable goldfield.

During the frenzied search for gold "Down Under," two prospectors, John Deason and Richard Oates, suddenly found their wagon stuck in the mud, blocked by a buried rock. Wearily, they began to dig out the obstruction, when their shovels uncovered an amazing sight — bright yellow metal gleaming through the mud. Clearing away the dirt, the two men gazed in awe at an enormous nugget of gold. Weighing 2,280 ounces, the nugget yielded an incredible 2,248 ounces of gold! Valued at more than $1,000,000, at current market values, the "Welcome Stranger" nugget is the largest ever discovered. Just three years later, in 1872, an enormous lump of gold interlaced with quartz was discovered at New South Wales. It had a combined weight of 10,080 ounces and yielded an unbelievable 7,560 ounces of gold! Value at today's prices — $3,780.000.

Meanwhile, as gold production increased in California, prospectors began to widen their search. In 1859 the Comstock Lode, a rich vein of ore containing silver and gold, was discovered in the Virginia Range of western Nevada, at the site of Virginia City. Production from the Comstock boomed for the next 20 years, then began to decline in the latter part of the 19th century. Eventually the finest-grade ore was exhausted, and the lode ceased producing. Even so, the mines along the three miles of the fault have yielded more than $400,000,000 in gold and silver since 1859.

In 1858 gold was discovered in Cherry Creek (in what is now downtown Denver) by a party of prospectors led by Russel Green. By the spring of 1859 the Colorado gold rush was at its height. Later that year, John Gregory made an even richer strike at Clear Creek, and nearby Central City promptly became a boomtown. Mining towns also flourished at Hamilton, Golden, Colorado City, and Boulder. But, but 1861, the gold rush was over, and thousands of luckless men vacated the mountains.

Colorado's economic difficulties received a much needed shot in the arm in the 1890s when new deposits were discovered at Cripple Creek. For many years, Cripple Creek was one of the world's leading gold-mining regions, producing more than $400,000,000 in gold since the first strike in 1891.

Montana's settlement came about as a direct result of a gold strike at Gold Creek in 1852. Henry Thomas sank the first shaft there in 1860, but it was not until two years later, when strikes were made on Grasshopper Creek, that the gold rush began in earnest. Nearby Bannack, the first of the boomtowns, had a population of about 1,000 early in 1864. Virginia City, founded on the site of a sizeable 1863 strike, promptly soared to a city of about 10,000. Hundreds of miners, many of them veterans of the American Civil War, poured into Montana. In 1867, steamboats on the Missouri carried 10,000 passengers to Fort Benton, the head of navigation, from whence they went along the Mullen Wagon Road to the mining districts. By the 1870s there were 500 gold camps in Montana.

Late in 1860, gold was discovered at Pierce, in the Nez Perce country, and, subsequently, thousands of miners sought their fortunes in the mining camps along the Clearwater and Salmon rivers and near present-day Boise. In three short years, Idaho's white population mushroomed from almost nothing to more than 20,000. The gold rush lasted for only a few short years, but the mining communities provided a basis for permanent settlement.

During the summer of 1874, a military expedition under Gen. George

(Top left) Gen. George Custer. After a patrol under his command verified reports that gold was plentiful in the Black Hills, eager miners swarmed into the area. (Top right) Sitting Bull. The invasion of the Black Hills by whites was a treaty violation, and when the American government failed to purchase the mineral rights from the Indians, Sitting Bull led his warriors against Custer in the battle at the Little Big Horn. (Below) This photograph shows Custer's last parade before the annihilation of his troops by Sitting Bull and his warriors.

Custer confirmed reports that the Black Hills in southwestern South Dakota were rich in gold. By mid-summer of 1875, hundreds of eager miners evaded military patrols to prospect the Black Hills, in violation of the Treaty of Fort Laramie of 1858. Concerned for the safety of the prospectors, the American government tried to negotiate with the Indians in an attempt to purchase mineral rights. Negotiations failed and war broke out, although most of the fighting, including the famous massacre of Custer's troops, occurred outside South Dakota.

In October the American government withdrew its troops from the area, giving tacit permission for prospectors to enter. Gold-seekers poured into the area, and, by the spring of 1876, some 15,000 miners had invaded the Black Hills. In the next year the population rose to about 25,000, with mining settlements such as Custer and Deadwood becoming turbulent, lawless communities.

Within a few years of the initial rush, most of the mining was being carried out by mining companies rather than individuals.

There has always been controversy regarding the first discoveries of gold in British Columbia. Some records indicate that gold was first procured from Indians at Fort Kamloops as early as 1852. Gov. James Douglas, in his diary, credits an Indian with discovering gold on the banks of the Nicomen River in 1856, while getting a drink of water. Regardless, in February, 1858, the steamer *Otter* sailed into San Francisco with 800 ounces of gold from the Fraser River. Californians, frustrated by the demise of their own gold rush, were intensely interested in this new source of gold, and that spring a small party set out for the region. They made a strike at Hill's Bar, named in honour of the discoverer, which eventually proved to be the richest ever found, yielding $2,000,000. When word of their success was carried back to San Francisco, hopeful gold-seekers stampeded to the area.

On April 25, 1858, the paddle wheel steamer *Commodore* docked at Fort Victoria with 450 men on their way to the Fraser River. She was followed by numerous others, and in May, June and July, an estimated 31,000 people arrived from San Francisco via land and sea.

Late in the fall of 1860, John Rose, Ben McDonald, "Doc" Keithley and George Weaver made a discovery 20 miles from Keithley Creek that would change the course of history of the Cariboo. That winter, more than 400 miners camped in the snow, waiting for spring thaw. Official yield for 1861 was $2,500,000, although unofficial estimates range as high as $5,000,000.

In the summer of 1862, a sailer named Billy Barker entered the Cariboo. Unable to find unstaked ground, he decided to try below the canyon on Williams Creek, much to the amusement of everyone. But the laughter ceased when, at the 52-foot mark of his shaft, Barker struck pay dirt. And what pay dirt — his claim eventually yielding $600,000.

Others now focused their attention on the area. Among them was John "Cariboo" Cameron, whose claim became the richest in the Cariboo. During 1863 it averaged from 120 to 336 ounces of gold per

day, with a lifetime output of nearly $1,000,000 — at a time when gold was worth less than $20 an ounce!

Around the claims of John Cameron and Billy Barker grew the boomtowns of Cameronton and Barkerville, the latter being declared "the largest community west of Chicago and north of San Francisco," and heralded as the "gold capital of the world."

The Cariboo did indeed prove to be of almost unbelievable richness, with numerous individual claims yielding fortunes in the precious metal. The Caledonia and Neversweat claims on Williams Creek yielded $750,000 and $120,000 respectively; Butcher's Bench ($125,000), Forest Rose ($480,000), and Prairie Flower ($100,000) being but a few others.

In 1865, the creeks were still yielding more than $3,000,000 annually. But the shallow diggings were becoming exhausted, and the day of the individual miner was ending. Most of the prospectors began searching for new discoveries, and eventually strikes in the Omineca, Peace, Cassiar and Atlin districts were explored and mined.

In 1864, Vancouver Island experienced its own gold rush when nuggets were discovered in the Leech River, a short distance from Victoria. Men promptly flooded the area, anticipating another great goldfield like those of California and the Cariboo; but the Leech River reserves proved to be limited. Mining operations soon petered out, with the prospectors seeking more promising areas.

The next significant gold discoveries were made in 1884 in South Africa. This time, however, there was no gold rush. This was due to the nature of the African deposits, where, instead of nuggets or dust, the reserves were in the form of a huge gold-bearing reef which extended well below the surface. This meant sizeable investment was needed to sink shafts, build mines and set up mills. The growth of the gold industry in Africa was slow but certain, and the richest in all of history.

Presently some 50 mines work about 4,000,000 cubic feet of rock daily, along a 300 mile arc. Hundreds of thousands of men, 90 percent of whom are low-paid Bantu-speaking tribesmen, descend 12,000 feet below ground and work at temperatures as high as 129 degrees Fahrenheit to extract the precious metal. By 1968 some $20,000,000,000 worth of gold had been extracted from the amazing Rand mine alone.

As early as the 1870s, prospectors were searching the Yukon for gold. However, it was the famous strike made on August 17, 1896, by George Carmack, Skookum Jim and Tagish Charlie, on a stream later renamed Bonanza Creek, that ignited the Klondike gold rush. On July 15, 1897, the *Excelsior* steamed into San Francisco Harbour with more than a ton of gold aboard. Two days later the steamship *Portland*

(Opposite page) Barkerville, named in honour of Billy Barker (inset), was located on the bank of Williams Creek, between Cameronton and Richfield, in the very heart of the Cariboo gold country. It was declared the largest community west of Chicago and north of San Francisco.

(Above) Robert Henderson c1898. It was because of his efforts that George Carmack (right) came to make the discovery on Bonanza Creek that touched off the Klondike gold rush. (Below) Rupert's claim on Cheechako Hill on Bonanza Creek, opposite the Discovery claim. Millions in raw gold was taken out of this small creek following the discovery there in 1896.

docked in Seattle with an additional two tons — bringing one of the greatest and richest goldfields ever known to the attention of the civilized world. But this was only the beginning. During August, September and October, steamer after steamer brought back men with sacks or valises full of precious yellow metal, until $2,500,000 had been taken out and placed into circulation. Within a year of the initial discovery, $5,500,000 had been recovered on Eldorado and Bonanza creeks alone.

Spurred by the over-dramatization of American and foreign newspapers, which tended to paint an unrealistic picture of creeks literally knee-deep in gold, thousands upon thousands rushed to the Klondike. From 1897 to 1899 approximately 100,000 adventurers journeyed to the region to seek their fortunes. For most it became a struggle for survival against a harsh environment, rather than a quest for golden wealth.

In the first decade, more than $100,000,000 in gold was mined around Dawson City, and the Yukon thrived. The Yukon was made a separate territory in 1898, with Dawson, then a town of almost 30,000, serving as capital. Then, as large mining companies brought complicated equipment to exploit the less accessible gold deposits, the placer miners began to leave. Gold valued at more than $22,000,000 was produced in the Klondike in 1900, the peak year. By 1910 most of the gold seekers had left the Yukon, and by the 1930s, Dawson's population had dwindled to about 1,000 people.

In the 1880s, Juneau and Treadwell, on the Alaska Panhandle, were founded as gold mining centres. The big bonanza, however, came after 1896, when gold deposits were discovered in the Klondike. Prospectors who failed to find locations there turned their attention to the possibilities of Alaska. They discovered gold at Nome (1899), Rampart, and Hot Springs, and the overflow from these camps rushed to the Fairbanks area, where a strike was made in 1902. Although gold continues to be produced in Alaska, principally in the Fairbanks area, the Yukon and Kuskowin River Valleys, and on the Seward Peninsula, production has steadily declined.

Thus it can be seen that the greatest period of activity in man's history — the vast gold discoveries in the United States, Australia, Canada, South Africa and Alaska — spanned only half a century.

Today gold is being mined on every continent in the world, at such exotic places as Fiji, Papua, Formosa, Japan and, as always, Egypt. During the early 1900s, the Philippines emerged as an important gold producer. Nearly all South American countries produce some gold, with Columbia being the leader.

Of the 65 gold-producing countries in the world today, South Africa is the acknowledged leader. For a brief period — 1814 to 1839 — Russia held sway as the world's leader in gold production, but has since fallen into second place, and is followed, respectively by Canada, the United States and Australia.

The largest gold-mining region in the world is the Witwatersrand

(Above) The first saloon in Dawson. Its receipts were said to have frequently reached 100 ounces of gold dust a day.
(Below) Dawson City, Yukon, at the height of the Klondike gold rush.

$1,500,000 in gold dust is shown here in the North American Transportation and Trading Company's warehouse in Dawson City.

goldfield extending 30 miles east and west of Johannesburg, South Africa. By 1944 more than 44 percent of the world's gold was mined there by 320,000 Bantu and 44,000 Europeans. By 1970, 76 percent of the world's gold was mined in this area. The largest gold mine is the East Rand Proprietary Mines Ltd., whose 8,785 claims cover 12,100 acres. The largest, measured by volume of ore extracted, is Randfontein Estates Gold Mine, with 170,000,000 cubic yards — enough to cover Manhattan Island to a depth of eight feet! The main tunnels, if placed end to end, would stretch for a distance of 2,600 miles.

As in everything else, Russia is highly secretive about her gold activities, but it is known that she is constantly seeking and mining gold. Russia has vast lode deposits in the trans-Baikal region east of Lake Baikal. Placer deposits have also been discovered in the Lena section of Siberia. The Ural Mountains' deposits are considered of low grade and costly to mine. The U.S.S.R. produced nearly 7,000,000 in 1971, and is estimated to be producing about 250 tons annually.

Since gold production was first officially recorded in 1858, Canada has produced 195,800,000 ounces to the end of 1972, valued at $6,436,000,000. Although most provinces have contributed to the total, Ontario, Quebec, British Columbia, the Yukon and Northwest Territories, in that order, have been the main producers.

The best gold producing year for Canada was recorded in 1941 when a record 5,345,179 ounces valued at $205,789,302 were mined. Since the Second World War the greatest annual production was reached in 1960, when 4,628,911 ounces were produced. Since 1961 Canadian gold production has been on a downward slide which continues each year; at least as recently as 1972, the last year for which production figures were available.

All gold produced in the Atlantic provinces in 1972 was recovered as a byproduct of base metal mining. Gold production from the large Ming ore body of Consolidated Rambler Mines Ltd. was largely responsible for the increase to 17,000 ounces, compared to 7,341 ounces in 1971.

Gold production in Quebec in 1972 amounted to 567,000 ounces compared with 646,839 in 1971. Although this represents a decrease of 12.3 percent, Quebec still remained the second highest gold-producing province, accounting for 27.3 percent of the national total. Five gold mines operated in the province in 1972: Chibougamau, Rouyn, Noranda, Malartic, and Val-d-Or.

Gold occurs widely across northern Ontario and has been mined on a large scale since 1910. Among the early important fields that are still major producers are those in the Porcupine area near Timmins; the Kirkland Lake fields, near the southeastern edge of the Great Clay belt of Ontario; and Larder Lake, at the Quebec border. Longlac, north of Lake Superior and east of Lake Nipigon, has been a significant producer of gold since 1934.

Ontario's gold production dropped, from 1,133,987 ounces in 1971, to an estimated 1,008,000 ounces in 1972. Gold production from lode mining accounted for 92.1 percent of the provincial total. Even though the overall production decreased by 10.1 percent from the previous year, Ontario continued as the leading gold-producing province, accounting for 48.5 percent of the national total. Eleven mines were in production in the province in 1972; four in the famed Porcupine mining district.

Virtually all gold produced in the Prairie provinces was recovered as a byproduct of base-metal ores. Production in 1972 was estimated at 71,000 ounces, compared to 56,023 ounces in 1971.

With the exception of a minor amount of gold recovered from

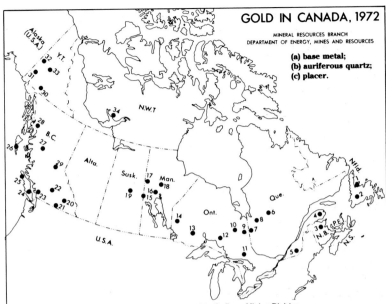

GOLD IN CANADA, 1972

MINERAL RESOURCES BRANCH
DEPARTMENT OF ENERGY, MINES AND RESOURCES

(a) base metal;
(b) auriferous quartz;
(c) placer.

Newfoundland
1   Consolidated Rambler Mines Limited (a)
2   American Smelting & Refining Co. (a)

New Brunswick
3   Heath Steele Mines Limited (a)

Quebec
4   Gaspe Copper Mines Ltd. (a)
5   Sullivan Mining Group Ltd. (a)
6   Chibougamau District:
    Campbell Chibougamau Mines (a)
    Falconbridge Copper Limited (a)
    Patino Mines (Quebec) Limited (a)
7   Noranda-Rouyn District:
    Falconbridge Copper Limited (a)
    Noranda Mines Limited (a)
    Malartic District:
    Camflo Mines Limited (b)
    East Malartic Mines Limited (a)
    Marban Gold Mines Limited (b)
    Bourlamaque-Louvicourt Dist.:
    Lamaque Mining Co. Ltd. (b)
    Manitou-Barvue Mines Ltd. (b)
    Sigma Mines (Quebec) Ltd. (b)
    Duparquet District:
    Kerr Addison Mines Limited (a)

Ontario
9   Larder Lake Mining Division:
    Hollinger Mines Ltd. (Ross) (b)
    Kerr Addison Mines Limited (b)
    Upper Beaver Mines Limited (b)
    Willroy Mines Limited (Macassa Division) (b)
10 Porcupine Mining Division:
    Auror Gold Mines Limited (b)
    Dome Mines Limited (b)
    McIntyre Porcupine (a) (b)
    Pamour Porcupine Mines Ltd. (b)

11 Sudbury Mining Division:
    Falconbridge Nickel Mines (a)
    The International Nickel Co. of Canada, Ltd. (a)
12 Noranda Mines (Geco Mine) (a)
13 Mattabi Mines Limited (a)
14 Campbell Red Lake Mines (b)
    Dickenson Mines Limited (b)
    Madsen Red Lake Gold Mines (b)
    Robin Red Lake Mines Ltd. (b)

Manitoba
15 Hudson Bay Mining and Smelting Co., Ltd. (a)
16 Sherritt Gordon Mines, Ltd. (Fox Lake) (a)
18 The International Nickel Co. of Canada, Ltd. (a)

Saskatchewan
19 Anglo-Rouyn Mines Ltd. (a)

British Columbia
20 Cominco Ltd. (a)
21 The Grandby Mining Co. Ltd. (a)
22 Bethlehem Copper Corp. (a)
    Brenda Mines Limited (a)
    Lornex Mining Corp. Ltd. (a)
    Similkameen Mining Co. Ltd. (a)
23 Texada Mines Ltd. (a)
24 Western Mines Ltd. (a)
25 Coast Copper Co. Ltd. (a)
    Utah Mines Ltd. (Island Copper Mine) (a)
26 Wesfrob Mines Ltd. (a)
27 Granisle Copper Ltd. (a)
    Nadina Explorations Ltd. (a)
    Noranda Mines Limited (Bell Copper) (a)
28 Granduc Operating Co. (a)
29 Gibralter Mines Ltd. (a) (c)

Yukon Territory
30 Whitehorse Copper Mines (a)
31 32 33   Small placer operations (c)

Northwest Territories
34 Cominco Ltd. (Con Mines) (b)

Although the great Hastings County gold rush in Ontario did not amount to much, small amounts of gold was produced. Shown in the photograph is the sluice end of the gold stamp mill.

placer deposits in the central part of the province and in the Atlin district, all gold produced in British Columbia was recovered as a byproduct of base-metal mines; mainly from the treatment of copper ores. The total gold production in 1972 was 121,000 ounces, compared to 65,760 in 1971. This represents 5.8 percent of the national total and made British Columbia the third largest gold-producing province in 1972, only because the Northwest Territories is not a province.

The Yukon reported a sharp decrease in gold production in 1972. Placer gold was produced by small operators in the Dawson, Mayo and Kluane districts.

In 1933, gold was discovered on the shores of Yellowknife Bay, on the northern arm of Great Slave Lake, in the Northwest Territories. In 1972 the Northwest Territories produced 13.9 percent of the national total, making it the third largest gold-producing "territory" that year. Five gold mines, all located near the town of Yellowknife, were in production, but the overall yield was lower than in 1971.

It should be pointed out that these Canadian gold production totals to 1972 generally pertain only to large mining operations, and do not include the totals accumulated by individuals. It is also well to note that the highest price paid in 1972 was $70 an ounce, reached in August of that year. Since then, uncertainties in the world monetary arrangements have led to a sharp rise in the price of gold on the open market. Currently (June 1991), the price is fluctuating around $450 an ounce. But is has reached $800 and many predict it will soon pass the $2,000 mark — a plateau once considered unattainable. This increase in price will stimulate the gold mining industry, encouraging new discoveries and reopening old mines once considered uneconomical. As a result, higher production, both in ounces and monetary value, is expected for the 1990s and beyond.

California, as one might expect, is the leading gold-producing state, with a production of 106,130,214 ounces from 1848 to 1965. In the early years, the rich placer deposits yielded phenomenal wealth. But, as they were depleted, prospectors searching for the source of placer gold found the highly productive gold-quarts veins of the Mother Lode and Grass Valley.

Colorado ranks second among the gold-producing states with an output of 40,755,923 ounces from the time of the initial discovery in 1858, through 1965.

South Dakota, with a production of 31,207,892 ounces from 1874 to 1965, is the third largest gold-producing state. The principal source of gold in the United States is the Homestake Mine in South Dakota, which, since beginning operations in 1879, has produced more than $1,000,000,000 in gold. The Homestake, which is more than a mile deep, yields about 575,000 ounces a year.

The Carlin Mine, near Carlin, Nevada, was opened in 1965, and is considered the largest gold discovery of the past 50 years. Its reserves are estimated at $700,000,000.

Some other leading gold-producing states, with production figures up to 1965, are: 4th — Alaska (29,872,981), 5th — Nevada (27,475,395), 6th — Utah (17,765,288), 7th — Montana (17,752,093) and 8th — Arizona (13,321,176).

CHAPTER TWO

Some Facts About Gold

FOR more than 6,000 years, gold has fascinated Man. It has been the root of conquests, tragedies, enslavements and countless deaths. The Egyptians, Arabs and Romans despoiled Africa and Asia Minor in their continued quest for gold. The Spanish Conquistadors raped and plundered South America and parts of the United States for it. Demand for gold has sent Roman legions to Britain, Portuguese sailors around Africa to the Orient, Columbus to the New World, forty-niners to California, and sourdoughs to Australia, Alaska and the Yukon.

But why does gold have such a mystical power over Man? Why is it held in such high esteem and sought by so many? Why does the mere mention of the word "gold" fire the imagination of the most complacent individual? Or, as someone so aptly put it, "Who ever heard of a silvery opportunity, or a heart of platinum?" To answer these questions, we must start at the beginning and examine some basic facts about gold.

Scientists believe that gold originated from a combination of gases and liquids deep within the molten core of the earth, millions of years ago. Throughout the ages it was slowly forced to the surface, together with silica solutions, through cracks or faults in the earth's crust. These "leaks" hardened to form the "veins" or "mother lode," as we know them today.

The scientific symbol for gold is "Au," derived from the latin *aurum,* which is itself derived from the Greek goddess of dawn, Aurora. Pure gold is a bright, glittering, brass-yellow colour, and is the most malleable, or workable, of all metals.

Gold is frequently referred to as a "noble" metal because it is chemically inactive, and is neither corroded by moisture nor affected by oxygen or ordinary acids. Gold's amazing resistance to sea water was verified by treasure hunter Alex Storm, who, with two compan-

Alchemists became obsessed with their quest for the secret of transmutation, motivated not only by the universal desire to increase material wealth, but equally by the belief that the solution was also the secret of restoring youth to man. Gold was eternal, and they desired the same promise.

ions, located the French pay ship *Le Chameau,* off Nova Scotia, in 1965. After being submerged in salt water for 240 years, the silver coins were badly corroded and fused together in clumps. However, the gold coins were still glittering and in perfect condition.

However, although gold is not affected by ordinary acids, it will react to chlorine and other halogens (fluoride, bromine, iodine, etc.), and can be dissolved by *aqua regia,* a mixture of nitric and hydrochloric acid which liberates chlorine, and by selenic acid.

Gold is eternal. Gold that was mined 6,000 years ago is still with us today, although, invariably, in the form of ingots, coinage, jewellery or some lost treasure trove. That very wedding band you so proudly display may once have been part of some exquisite ancient gold work.

In the Middle Ages, an ancient system of science and magic was devoted to the transmutation, or changing, of substances from one form into another. This ancient "science," the beginning of modern chemistry, was called alchemy. The major goal of alchemists was to transmute lead, and other base metals, into gold. Alchemists believed that all metals were composed of sulphur and mercury in different proportions, and that by altering the proportions of each, they could change the metal into gold. This was supposed to be achieved with the assistance of a "philosopher's stone," made from many formulas, but always containing salt, mercury and sulphur. If the stone contained red sulphur, the metal was supposedly changed to gold; white sulphur — silver. Alchemical apparatus included the alembic (or ambix) for distillation and the kerotakis for sublimation.

Alchemy probably originated in Egypt about 300 BC. From Egypt, it was adopted in the Middle East, and then western Europe. Although Alchemy was more widely practiced during the Middle Ages, it survived until the 18th century. Alchemists became obsessed with their quest for the secret of transmutation, motivated not only by the universal desire to increase material wealth, but equally by the belief that the solution was also the secret to restoring youth to men. They believed that gold was the elixir of life, which could cure all illnesses, prolong life, and even make man immortal. Gold was eternal, and they desired the same promise for themselves.

Today the atom-smasher can convert lead into gold by bombarding it with protons and neutrons. It can also create an unstable form of gold from both platinum and iridium. However — ironically — gold from lead is currently too expensive to produce, and platinum and iridium are more valuable in their own form.

Gold is a relatively soft metal, with a rating on Mohs scale of 2.5 — about the same substance as a fingernail. It is also extremely ductile. An ounce of gold can be drawn, in the form of continuous thread, to a length of about 35 miles! A cubic inch of gold can be hammered into gold leaf four-millionths of an inch thick, so as to cover nearly 1,400 square feet! Gold used in certain gilding processes is usually purchased in books of 25 leaves, each about 3¼ inches square and approximately 1/200,000 of an inch thick. The gold is first alloyed with silver or copper in proportions that vary according to the desired colour of the gilding. The alloy is melted, cast into ingots, rolled, annealed, then cut into small squares which are hammered between sheets of vellum. These are twice quartered and re-beaten between sheets of goldbeater's-skin, a membrane from the intestine of oxen. The extreme thinness to which gold can be beaten without disintegrating is said to be about 1/300,000 of an inch thick. These gold leaves are so incredible thin that light can actually pass through them, the colour emitted dependent upon fineness. Gold leaf of 23 carats, for example, will transmit a greenish light; 18 carat, a blue light; 16 carat, a pale blue light, etc.

Gold has many uses. It was first moulded into crude trinkets, then crafted into fine jewellery. In the 18th century BC, the first gold coins were introduced in Lydia in Asia Minor and in China. They were composed of a natural alloy of gold and silver, called electrum. By the end of the 6th century, gold coins were minted in many Greek city-states. Today, gold is a generally accepted means of balancing international accounts and is the favoured metal for backing currency. Many countries, Africa, Canada and the United States being the leaders, produce 999.9 fine bullion coins in one ounce sizes down to 1/10 ounce for individuals who may wish to own pure gold.

As mentioned, gold can be spread extremely thin, permitting light to pass through, yet effectively reflecting a large portion of the sun's scorching infrared rays. This feature makes it invaluable as a coating for office windows, allowing people to see through, but not allowing much heat to enter. This reduces the power needed to operate air conditioning equipment, and, thereby, conserves energy. For the same reasons gold is used on the plastic visors worn by astronauts.

Gold can also be processed so as to be soluble in oil. When such a mixture is applied to glass, and the glass is heated, the oil burns off, leaving a film of pure gold only five-millionths of an inch thick. That's how gold letters and designs are applied to such items as glasses and tumblers. Because gold is such a fine conductor of electricity, and because it does not corrode, much is used in tiny but dependable circuitry for pocket calculators, television sets, computers and other scientific and electronic apparatus. Gold compounds are used in chemistry, photography, and many other fields. Gold is also used to replace teeth, although, at today's prices, we may have seen the last golden fillings!

As in ancient times, however, by far the greatest use of gold is in the manufacture of jewellery.

Many beginning prospectors and gold panners are often confused between gold and pyrite. Pyrite, a pale brass-yellow mineral is a bisulphide of iron. It occurs most commonly in crystals (belonging to the isometric system and usually produced in the form of cubes and pyritohedons), but is also found in massive, granular and stalactite form. The only similarly between gold and pyrite is the colour, as pyrite lacks all the properties of gold. While gold can be hammered

(Above) The stuff dreams are made of — gold!
(Below) An iron pyrite cube. Because of its brass-yellow colour, pyrite is frequently mistaken for gold. However, pyrite is brittle, while gold is very malleable.

into fantastically thin sheets, pyrite will crumble when hammered. Therefore, if you find a yellow metal of which you are uncertain, simply pound it with a rock or hammer. If it crumbles into dust it is not gold. Despite the name "fool's gold," however, pyrite often does contain gold of which auriferous pyrite is a commercially important source. Also, pyrite itself is not worthless, but is mined, processed and used in the manufacturer of sulphuric acid and refrigerator fluid.

Since gold is soft, it must be hardened by alloying it with copper, silver, or some other metal. White gold, a substitute for platinum, is an alloy of gold with platinum, palladium, nickel or nickel and zinc. When more than 20 percent silver is present, the alloy is called electrum. Alloys of gold with copper are a reddish-yellow and are used for coinage and jewellery. Green alloys are formed by adding silver and cadmium to gold, while a purple alloy is obtained by adding aluminium.

The gold content of an alloy is commonly stated in carats, a carat representing 1/24 part by weight of the total mass. Pure gold, therefore, is 24 carats. Pure gold is designated as being 1000 fine (100 percent). Thus gold containing 10 percent of other metals is only 90 percent pure, and is said to have a fineness of .900, i.e. 900/1000 parts gold and 100/1000 parts other metals. Gold from different regions of the globe will vary greatly in fineness. Australian gold reaches .995 in certain area, the purest found in the natural state, while South American gold is only .650 fine. Gold from California's mother lode may reach .900 fine or better, while some Canadian gold reaches .980 fine. Refining processes are used to separate and to purify the gold; once these processes have been completed all gold is exactly alike.

Most gold is found in the form of dust, flakes or nuggets. It is seldom found in the pure state, and usually occurs in association with silver, or other metals, in quartz veins or lodes so finely disseminated that it is not visible. It also is found in alluvial placer deposits, which are worked by panning, dredging or hydraulic mining. In mining gold, two steps are necessary, regardless of the type of deposit. Gold must be extracted from its ores by mechanical means, and separated from the other metals by chemical process; notably the flotation process, the amalgamation process or the cyanide process. (These will be discussed in a later chapter.) Gold also occurs in compounds, notable the telluride. Ores containing as little as $1 worth of gold per ton can be worked economically by using chemical methods of extraction.

In summary then, gold is found: (1) in lode deposits, (2) in placer deposits, (3) in porphyry copper as a minor element, and (4) in sea water. Lode deposits are "veins" in the rocks and earth's crust. Placer deposits are found in the beds of streams and rivers, and consists of grains and nuggets. These nuggets were washed from the so-called lode by water, wind and erosion, and carried downstream. The greatest untapped reserves of gold in the world today lie in the world's oceans, where billions of tons are dissolved. Although this has long been common knowledge, no one has yet developed an economical

These miners are examining a rich vein of gold at the 700-foot level of the Coniaurum mine, Scumacher, Ontario. Due to the large investment required for hardrock mining, the individual was quickly eliminated. Prospectors who discover lode deposits usually sell or lease the mining rights to a large, well-equipped mining company.

way of extracting it. In the 1920s a German scientist named Fritz Haber invented a filtering apparatus to separate gold from sea water. But after four years of operation the system was abandoned as uneconomical.

The next time you become discouraged in your search for gold, or someone tells you there's no gold in "them thar hills," remember this: *To date man has only secured about .00002 of 1 percent of the total gold in the earth's crust!*

CHAPTER THREE

How To Locate Placer Gold

I N the first chapter, I gave a brief description of most of the world's important gold rushes or discoveries. If you reside in or near an area of historic activity, consider yourself fortunate. However, one should not get too excited simply because he/she is in or near an area where gold was once discovered and mined. For, regardless of how great the original discovery was, proximity to the area, in itself, does not guarantee success. A great deal of effort must still be expended when in the mineral-rich zone. The gold, after all, will not simply be laying loose on the surface waiting for someone to scoop it up. In fact, if the area was previously worked it will be exceedingly more difficult to find paying ground than it was when the original prospectors worked there. But, while early prospectors had the advantage of being first, modern prospectors have the advantage of superior gold-recovery equipment, thus permitting previously-worked areas to be reworked properly. However, even equipment capable of recovering 100 percent of the gold from the gravel it processes would be worthless, if there was no gold in the gravel being processed. Where then, do you begin your search? Obviously, some clues and background information would be extremely helpful.

The major gold-producing regions of North America are well known. In the United States it includes most of the western states, a few southeastern states, and Alaska. In Canada, Ontario, Quebec, British Columbia and the Yukon are the areas of greatest activity, although there have been gold rushes in other provinces as well. To find gold, the prospector must first go to where gold has historically been discovered. The exact localities of gold mining in Canada and the United States, covered in general in Chapter 1, can be located on detailed mining maps, and specific information is usually available from respective department of mines in the various provinces or states. For the general areas of British Columbia goldfields, consult the map on the next page.

(NOTE: My companion book, *Methods of Placer Mining,* contains a chapter entitled "Gold Rushes of the World." This chapter contains information on gold discoveries in: Alabama, Alaska, Australia, British Columbia, California, Colorado, Georgia, Idaho, Montana, Nevada, New Mexico, North Carolina, Virginia, Washington and the Yukon.)

By concentrating your search on areas that have produced gold in the past your chances for success are much greater than if you wandered aimlessly about. Remember, the chances of a major new discovery are extremely remote, as most areas have been thoroughly searched by hundreds of prospectors over the years. Remember, also, that you are following a parade of hundreds — even thousands — of professional prospectors and miners, including the thorough Chinese, who remained and worked the claims long after the whites had departed. And, due to the tremendous increase in the price of gold today, more amateurs are trying their luck than ever before.

Before venturing into a certain region in search of gold, it is a good idea to do some research into the history of that area's gold-bearing creeks. Did they produce flour gold, or flakes and nuggets? Did the stream produce consistently for several years, or was it merely a small local discovery? And last, but certainly not least, is it readily accessible to the modern prospector?

My previously mentioned book *Methods of Placer Mining* should be extremely helpful in answering these questions, as far as British Columbia is concerned. In it you will find a brief history of most of British Columbia's placer creeks, as well as the prospects for the modern gold seeker. There are others, of course, and a visit to your local library would be a good way to begin your search; not to mention a good book store.

Finding and panning gold requires hard work, knowledge and patience. You will likely be competing with other amateur, and professional, prospectors, so the more determined and educated your search, the greater your chances of being successful. Once you have chosen an area that has a good gold-bearing history, the next thing to do is to get as far as possible from the main roads. Like fishing, the best spots are those which are least accessible, as they are less likely to have been worked over, especially by the hordes of modern prospectors who are now invading the field. Once you have reached a promising creek, your knowledge of gold, as outlined in this book, will give you a great advantage.

Although the modern gold panner need not acquire a profound knowledge of geology, he/she should have a clear understanding of the nature and characteristics of gold, as well as how it originated.

Gold originated in the depths of the earth, where it was formed by some unknown process millions of years ago. Volcanic activity released gold and other elements, which in a gaseous or liquid form, was forced upward by titanic pressure and tremendous heat. Because of its fluid nature, gold was forced into the cracks, pores and fissures

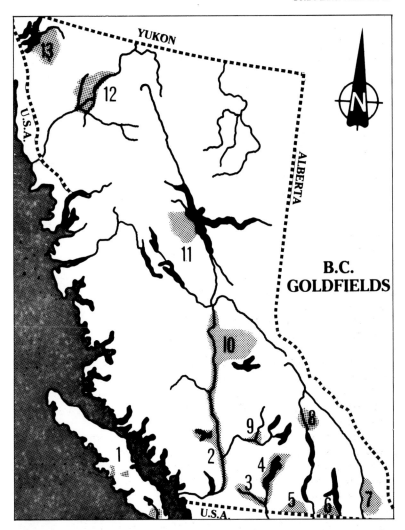

BRITISH COLUMBIA GOLDFIELDS

1. Vancouver Island
2. Fraser River
3. Simalkameen
4. Okanagan
5. Boundary Country
6. West Kootenay
7. East Kootenay
8. Big Bend
9. Thompson
10. Cariboo
11. Omineca
12. Cassiar
13. Atlin

NOTE: Information on the history of B.C. placer creeks, along with its current potential as a gold producer, is available in *Methods of Placer Mining*, a new book by Garnet Basque. A series detailed placer creek maps is also included.

Fig. 1
TYPES OF PLACER DEPOSITS

1. RESIDUAL PLACER
2. ELUVIAL PLACER
3. BENCH PLACER
4. STREAM PLACER

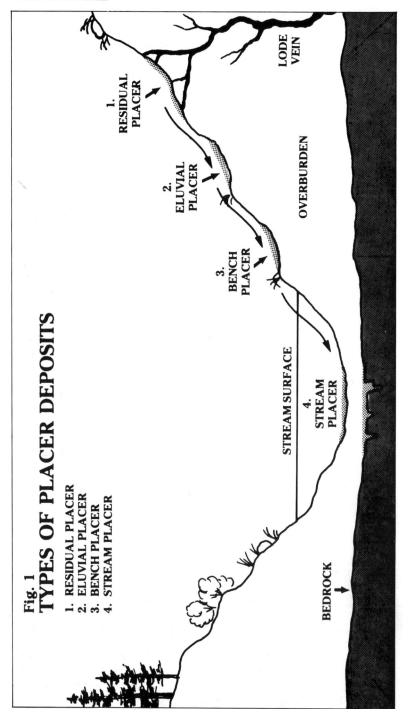

of rocks. Some of these cracks are so minute that they can only be detected by a microscope, while others form massive veins or lodes. This process occurred between 2,000,000 and 10,000,000 years ago.

As the gold cooled, it solidified into the form of these veins, sometimes in combination with other metals. These original veins are called lodes, and are the principal source of all gold. Gold is most commonly associated with milk-white quartz, which has been termed "the home of gold." It is most frequently found in eruptive rocks and veins, intrusions and overflows in the metamorphic strata.

Nature did not create placer deposits as she did lodes, but placers are a direct result of lodes. Over the centuries these lodes were exposed to the grinding effect of glaciers, and the relentless effects of the elements — wind, rain and snow. It then expanded on freezing, gradually enlarging and deepening the cracks until, eventually, chunks were broken off. Throughout this whole process wind, rain, snow and other natural forces had been constantly working on the face of this rock mass. Earth tremors and rock slides also played an important part, further crushing and breaking up the veins. The resulting flakes and nuggets were then carried downhill by spring run-off until they reached a stream or river. Each spring nature replenishes her streams in this fashion. Placer deposits, then, are the results of decomposition and the wearing away of veins and lodes.

As you can see, therefore, there are only two ways in which gold can be commercially found — lodes and placers. Lodes are the original veins which are formed and worked intact, or deteriorates to form placers. Placers are deposits of sand, gravel or related material containing particles of gold or other valuable minerals in sufficient quantity to be of economic interest. Since lode mining generally employs large industrial machines and chemical processes, we will only touch upon its characteristics from time to time when discussing placer deposits. Placers, after all, are the primary interest of the gold panner or weekend prospector, requiring a minimum amount of equipment and capital to work.

Normally three conditions are necessary for the formation of commercial placers. First, quite naturally, there must be a vein or lode in the vicinity. Second, the original vein must be decomposed by natural elements and carried to a stream. Third, the gold-bearing material must be accumulated by stream or water action in sufficient quantities to make a mining venture worthwhile.

There are four principal types of placers (Fig. 1). As already explained, placer deposits are formed by natural concentration of the weathered gold-bearing vein. Residual placers are formed at the point of the weathered gold outcrop. Gold, being heavy and inert, tends to remain at or near its original source. Run-off water removes a relatively small amount of this material. The richness of a residual placer, therefore, depends upon the richness of the original lode. In British Columbia, residual placers are of little importance because rapid erosion has dispersed the parts of most lodes that have been weathered in preglacial times, particularly those parts lying in exposed positions above valley bottoms. Nevertheless, in the early prospecting for outcrops of gold-bearing veins in the Bridge River and Wells mining camps some residual concentrations were found and were worked as placers.

In the course of weathering, part of the lode is disintegrated and carried away by gravity or water action. Eluvial placers are formed by gold that has travelled as little as a few feet from the originating lode. On a high, steeply-sloped canyon, however, it is possible for an eluvial deposit to form several hundred feet below the originating vein, while still several hundred feet above the stream. (The opposite of eluvial is alluvial, which means gold has been carried many miles from its original source.)

A bench placer is nothing more than a stream placer that has been left high and dry by the stream that originally created it.

Stream placers are the most important to prospectors. In British Columbia placers are largely the result of stream concentration of one type or another. The disintegrating material from the original gold-bearing vein is gradually carried downhill until it reaches a stream channel. Here, the sorting action of running water results in small fragments and lighter materials being "floated" downstream. Meanwhile, the material in the stream bed is constantly being agitated, enabling the gold to work deeper into the gravel until it reaches bedrock, where the richest concentrations are likely to occur.

While the occurrence of placers would tend to indicate the existence of lodes nearby, this is not always the case. In the Klondike, for instance, where the placer gold was derived from gold-bearing quartz veins, no significant lode deposits have been found.

Gold is, by its very nature, irregularly distributed in placers. Generally, gold will migrate downward in sand or gravel as long as the material is loose and is agitated by flowing water. Coarse gold, frequently accompanied by some fine or moderately coarse gold, settles until it reaches bedrock. Consequently, the paystreak in many instances is on bedrock. However, gold may be scattered throughout the last several feet just above bedrock, especially if it contains much clay or compact material. If the downward motion of gold is stopped at a clay layer or bed of tightly packed gravel, a paystreak may be formed on what is termed false bedrock. This may occur some distance above the actual bedrock.

Since gold is seldom uniformly distributed through the gravel, the prospector is usually searching for a workable paystreak. In most bars and some bench deposits it is the upper gravel that is enriched while the lower material is low grade or barren. However, "paystreaks may occur at any elevation in a gravel deposit on a false bedrock of clay or other impervious bed. This may or may not occupy the deepest part of a stream channel. Pay gravel may occupy the whole width of the stream bottom in narrow, V-shaped valleys; in broad, flat-bottomed valleys the paystreak is likely to be much narrower than the valley floor and its course may be quite different from that of the present stream. Most paystreaks in broad valleys were originally formed in narrow valleys of fairly high gradients. As the gradient became less and the valley was widened by the meandering stream, the paystreak was buried beneath alluvium. A stream of low gradient tends to meander and the bends tend to move downstream, so that the materials in the valley bottom are reworked many times by the stream. A paystreak may be shifted in location by this process of reworking by the stream, or, if the deposit consists of coarse material or becomes somewhat cemented or hardened after the shifting of the stream, it may remain in its original position. Paystreaks are not continuous and may split or terminate abruptly, because gold is accumulated chiefly at such places as the insides of bends, where alternate deposition and erosion take place and where the bedrock forms good 'riffles.' Uplift or some other geological event may cause the stream to deepen its valley or remain in its original position to form a bench or old channel placer. Barren ground may occur, therefore, in the bottom of the present stream valley in the stretches that are bordered by one or more rock benches, and exceptionally rich ground may occur where the stream has cut down beneath the old channel.

"Pot-holes and other depressions in the bedrock or stream rarely contain gold. They are formed by erosion and gold carried into them by the stream is likely to be ground fine by the action of the current-transported sand and gravel and to be washed out. Gold does not occur in payable quantities in the submerged parts of deltas. Some gold may occur in alluvial fans that frequently form the upper parts of deltas, but only fine gold can occur in fans and there is little opportunity for its concentration into paystreaks because of frequent shifting of the stream channels.

"Flood (bar or fine) gold is sufficiently fine or flaky to be transported in muddy water. The particles range in size from a few to several thousand 'colours' to the cent. In regions where fine gold is supplied to the streams by erosion of their banks or beds, paystreaks may occur in the bars and banks of the streams. The paystreaks as a rule are only a few inches to a foot or two thick and lie in or near the surface between extreme low-water and high-water marks, in places (as on the upstream side of bars) where conditions are favourable for alternate deposition and erosion of material transported by the stream. They may occur in bench deposits at various elevations above the streams. As erosion and deposition go on from year to year the bars shift downstream; old paystreaks are destroyed and new ones formed, but at a very slow rate. The rich flood gold deposits mined in early days on the Fraser and on other streams in Canada represented the concentration of gold by these streams in post-glacial time. The placer deposits of the Saskatchewan and Athabasca rivers, in Alberta, as well as most of those along the Fraser, Stikine, and Columbia rivers in British Columbia, are of this type. Many of the richer bars on these streams have been worked several times. The first harvest, of course,

A gold dredge at work on the river near Edmonton, Alberta in 1898.

was the richest and the work in recent years has barely paid.

"Gravel-plain placers are formed in broad valleys or alluvial plains containing gravels that have been repeatedly re-worked by meandering streams or by streams of fairly high gradients that tend to shift their channels. The gold is derived by erosion of the banks and the land at the headwaters of the streams, and is likely to be moderately fine and fairly evenly distributed through the gravels. Such placers are best developed in unglaciated areas, but occur on a small scale in glaciated regions, for example, at a few places in Cariboo district, British Columbia. They can be profitable mined as a rule only by dredging.

"Glacial gravels may contain gold, but have little economic value unless they have been re-concentrated by stream action or have been derived in part by erosion of pre-existing placers. Glacial erosion is more likely to disperse earlier placers than to form concentrations of heavy minerals. Moraines, kames, eskers, and glacial outwash plains have not proved to contain gold in paying quantities. Scattered pieces of gold and isolated masses of gold-bearing gravels may occur in boulder clay. Stratified glacial silt and clay contain no gold. Interglacial paystreaks formed by normal stream erosion during a long interval between periods of glacial advance may occur in glaciated regions, in a place sheltered from the scouring of later glaciation. Much of the gold found in glacial gravels is moderately coarse and fairly uniform in size, as if sorted by powerful streams. The re-sorted glacial gravel placers of the old placer mining regions of British Columbia and of Beauceville district, Quebec, have been mined chiefly by hydraulicking and could barely be mined profitably in any other way.

"Buried placers are paystreaks that are covered with later deposits of glacial drift, lavas, and tuffs, or barren alluvium. Gold-bearing gravels, buried beneath great or small thicknesses of glacial drift, may occur in the bottoms of valleys or on rock benches and in old stream channels bordering valleys that were not severely glaciated. Such valleys are V-shaped. Rounded, U-shaped valleys are not likely to contain buried paystreaks, because of the effects of glacial erosion. Glacial gravels in the bottoms of such valleys may contain some gold, but the pay is generally so scattered that it cannot be mined profitably. Most of the rich paystreaks mined in early days in the Cariboo and in other districts in British Columbia were buried beneath glacial drift and were mined chiefly by drifting (tunnelling). Lava-buried placers have been found in only a few places in Canada, as at Ruby Creek in Atlin district, but other occurrences may be found in British Columbia and Yukon Territory. The rising of the base-level or erosion, or overloading of streams, may cause deposition of barren alluvium above the pay gravels in a valley bottom. In arctic and sub-arctic regions, as in the Klondike, the ground is permanently frozen and thick deposits of 'muck' commonly overlie the gravels. Muck consists of slightly decomposed organic matter mixed and interbedded with fine sand, silt, and clay. It is formed partly by growth of vegetation in place and by soil creep and partly by deposition from overflowing streams. In places it contains much 'ground ice' or permafrost. As muck is a good insulator, it prevents thawing of the ground during the summer. Ground from which the muck has been removed by hydraulicking or by some other method thaws naturally to depths of 10 to 30 feet in three or four years.

"Placers in the glaciated parts of Canada differ from those in the unglaciated parts of the Yukon in several ways that affect their mining possibilities. The presence of large boulders in some placers in the glaciated area renders the deposits workable only by the heaviest types of mechanical equipment. Bedrock in glaciated areas is likely to be hard and unweathered and this may make more difficult the recovery of all the gold by dredging, although modern dredges used in the Klondike successfully overcame this where the rock was jointed. Large boulders are absent and there is no overburden or glacial drift in the placers of the unglaciated parts of the Yukon. There are thick deposits of muck, however, and thawing of the ground is necessary in mining operations.

"The most favourable areas in Canada for prospecting for placers probably are any parts of the Yukon and northern•British Columbia that may not have been prospected exhaustively. Unglaciated areas in which mineral-bearing igneous or metamorphic rocks occur, at least to some extent, are the most favourable. In glaciated areas narrow, V-shaped valleys, preferably those bordered by rock benches, should be sought, and rounded, severely glaciated valleys avoided."

Beach placers are formed by a combination of the concentrating action of waves, tide and current upon gold-bearing sands and cliffs. Concentrations rich enough to be worked economically are rare, and considerable difficulty is often experienced in separating small, rusty flake gold from magnetic sand. In Canada, beach placers have been found at Wreck Bay (now called Florencia Bay), Vancouver Island, on the east coast of Graham Island and the north shore of the Gulf of St. Lawrence.

As one would expect, the mining of placer gold is normally the first gold-mining activity carried on in a country or region. This is because alluvial deposits are always the easiest to identify and work profitably. Contrary to what many people may have assumed, Canada's first important placer discovery did not occur in British Columbia. This distinction belongs to the basin of the Chaudiere River southeast of Quebec City. Although the initial discoveries were made in 1823, it was not until 1875 that extensive mining began. Some 500 miners were employed between the peak years of 1875-1885, when about $2,000,000 was mined. After 1885 the yield declined.

While the placer operations in Quebec were the only significant placer mines in eastern Canada, there have been other low-grade occurrences as well. Although these were never successfully exploited, the possibility of finding workable deposits in eastern Canada should not be overlooked.

Canada's greatest placer belt, however, lies in the Cordilleran region, discovered as a result of the northward push of prospectors from California. From British Columbia the argonauts pressed northward, eventually reaching and penetrating the Yukon and Alaska. The Klondike region is one of the few parts of Canada that was not glaciated, and thus was favourable for the occurrence of rich placers. It is significant to note that the relatively small unglaciated area in the Yukon has yielded nearly three times as much placer gold as has the remainder of Canada, which was glaciated.

The Peace and North Saskatchewan rivers in British Columbia and Alberta are the only other places in western Canada where placer mining has been done to any extent. A relatively small amount of fine-grained gold has been and is still being obtained from these rivers. The Peace River gold may have worked its way down from tributaries in the interior of British Columbia where lodes are known to occur, or it may have been concentrated from glacial gravels. The gold of the North Saskatchewan apparently came from the erosion of sedimentary rocks that contain slight amounts of gold.

Canada's principal placer region extends over much of British Columbia and the Yukon. Flanked by the Rocky Mountains on the east and the Coast Mountains on the west, this enormous mineral-rich zone extends through central British Columbia, continues into the central part of the Yukon and on into Alaska. Not only does this large region, pinnacled with fairly ancient mountains, contain numerous lodes whose weathering provided the gold that became concentrated in placers, but the topography was such that placers accumulated, largely protected from the effects of glaciation. Some ancient placers were preserved as old channels and covered by glacial debris or lava; others were scoured clean by glaciers, their golden deposits mingled with glacial drift and eventually re-concentrated by modern streams or rivers. These deposits were the source of the gold that provided impetus to the gold rushes of British Columbia, Yukon and Alaska. Parts of British Columbia, Yukon and Alaska are therefore the most favourable places in which to seek placers. The reader should be reminded, however, that much of the area has already been searched extensively, and, because of higher gold prices, many areas are being re-worked yet again. However, there is always the possibility of discovering some previously overlooked ground, or better still, an ancient stream bed. Such was the case in 1972 when, after years of persistence, the Toop family struck pay dirt on an ancient stream bed of Mary Creek in the Barkerville-Quesnel area. The find has been estimated at being worth from $7,000,000 to $15,000,000. (For those readers who would like to read the full account of this great modern-day discovery, the story can be found in *The Best of Canada West (Vol. 1)*, published by Stagecoach Publishing in 1978. The book is now out of print, but a copy should be available at most libraries.)

You should now be familiar with the types of placer deposits, how these deposits were formed, and the likely areas where they will

Fig. 2
PLACER DEPOSIT LOCATIONS

A. At the base of waterfalls.
B. Where obstructions hinder or halt its progress.
C. Trapped by the roots of plants.
D. In cracks and crevices in the bedrock.
E. In deep pools, or wherever the water velocity slows down.

NOTE: In all cases the gold, because of water agitation, will eventually migrate downward through the overburden to bedrock, where the richest deposits are normally found.

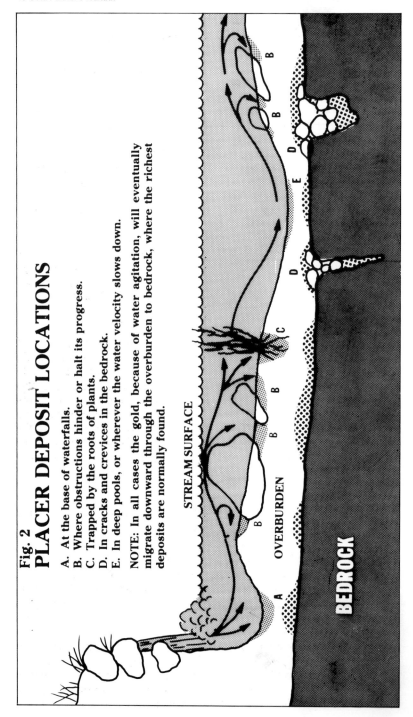

STREAM SURFACE

OVERBURDEN

BEDROCK

occur. The next thing you must learn is what happens to the gold *after* it enters a stream. One essential fact should always be uppermost on your mind when searching for placer gold — GOLD IS HEAVY. Because of this one singular fact, gold will accumulate at certain spots in a creek or stream after it has been carried there. Your ability to recognize these locations could be the difference between a long, tedious, unrewarded effort, and success. Regardless how impatient you may be to get started, you cannot merely approach a stream and begin panning indiscriminately — not if you really want to recover gold. Panning gold requires hard work, both mental and physical. Therefore, the first step upon reaching a promising creek is to proceed upstream to a high vantage point. From here you can study the area, and even take some photographs for later study. But most importantly, try to visualize the stream's high-water mark during the rainy season. Remember that gold carried downstream during the spring run-off may be deposited high and dry by summer, when you are most likely to begin your search. As you stand there, overlooking the creek, you must be able to visualize these six fundamental rules, remembering that they will also apply to spring run-off. So do not overlook these signs even if they are currently above the high-water mark.

☆ ☆ ☆

(1) GOLD IS HEAVY

Gold is extremely heavy, six or seven times heavier than rock, and therefore it settles on the bottom. The key work here is *down.* Gold's excessive weight forces it *down* — *down*hill, *down*stream, *down* into the sands and gravel, *down* into bedrock cracks and crevices, and *down* in your sluice box or gold pan. Gold is assisted in its *down*ward movement by wind, rain, earth tremor, rock slide and water agitation. Once gold settles on the creek bed, it will sift *down*ward through the lighter sand and gravel. Because of its weight, it will continue to sink until it reaches bedrock, where it will become trapped in crevices and such.

☆ ☆ ☆

(2) WATER VELOCITY

Because gold is heavy and sinks, it will concentrate wherever the creek slows down or loses sufficient velocity to drag it further downstream. In other words, if gold is dragged from a mountainside to a deep, motionless pool, it will immediately sink to the bottom. The first principle of prospecting for placer gold, then, is to search where the flow of water decreases. Therefore, pay special attention to the edges of whirlpools, at the tail of eddies, beneath waterfalls and in deeper pools. Fine gold is usually found in shallow areas, and coarse gold in deeper areas.

A popular misconception is that all nuggets sink immediately to the bottom at, or near, the spot they first enter a stream. This is generally true, but depends a great deal upon the size of the nuggets and the velocity of the water. For example, a stream flowing at only one-half mile per hour can lift and carry gravel about the size of a

Never overlook the possibilities of an uprooted tree, especially along the banks of a well known gold producing stream. Here the author examines long roots that could expose nuggets inaccessible by any other means.

pea. At five miles per hour, stones the size of cannon balls will tumble freely. When the velocity is slightly greater than 20 miles per hour, boulders that weigh nearly a ton can be moved gradually. And, during spring run-off, the velocity is often much greater than this.

☆ ☆ ☆

(3) OBSTRUCTIONS

Gold tends to be deposited at any point where obstructions hinder or halt its progress. Large rocks beneath the surface act as natural riffles and can accumulate rich pockets of placer gold. Likewise, a fallen tree trunk or other natural obstruction will impede the gold's progress, causing it to sink. If a tree trunk, embankment or other obstruction projects from the bank into the current, a suction eddy will likely be formed. It is these deep suction eddy pools that many of the richest "glory holes" have been found. However, these pools are usually deep, and may be accessible only through the use of scuba gear, underwater dredges, and the like.

☆ ☆ ☆

(4) SHORTEST DISTANCE BETWEEN TWO POINTS

Again, because of its weight, gold tends to take the shortest route as it is carried downstream. It therefore hugs the inside of bends and curves in its journey. Then, as these areas tend to lose velocity, the

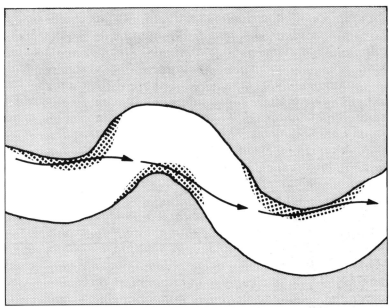

Because gold tends to take the shortest route as it is dragged downstream, it gathers in the inside curves where the water slows down.

gold sinks to the bottom. Quite often the suspended sand, silt, iron and gold particles will build up until a small drift of sand is formed. This type of deposit is easily recognizable above or below the water, and has accounted for many of the famous "gold bars" of past history. The strike at Hill's Bar, near Hope in 1858, which touched off the Fraser River gold rush, yielded nearly $2,000,000. Unfortunately, you cannot make much money trying to pan these sandbars Even a professional gold panner can only sift through about one cubic yard of gravel per day, so unless you are sluicing or dredging, stick to bedrock mining. You will save yourself a lot of wasted effort, sore muscles and discouragement.

☆　☆　☆

(5) BLACK SAND

Iron pyrites and black sands are good indications of gold. When these are spotted it is always a smart idea to prospect. Black sands are heavier than surrounding sand and settle much in the same manner as does gold. Therefore, if black sands are present, you can be assured that conditions are favourable for placer gold deposits. However, since this principle was well known to the early prospectors, it's almost certain that the most obvious black sand concentrations have already been panned. If this proves to be the case, modern technology may be very useful. A metal detector can determine the presence of gold and black sand deposits beneath the surface which went undetected by earlier prospectors. Some people search for small nuggets with a metal detector, and many have been successful. However, if

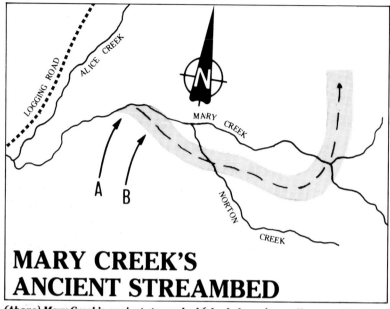

MARY CREEK'S
ANCIENT STREAMBED

(Above) Mary Creek's ancient stream bed (shaded area) was discovered by Terry Toop at point "A" in 1972, with coarse gold and nuggets found near point "B" (Below) A placer mining operation on Norton Creek in 1890. A tributary of Mary Creek, Norton Creek cut across the ancient stream bed.

you intend to search underwater, be certain you have a waterproof search coil.

☆   ☆   ☆

(6) ANCIENT STREAM BED

Over the tens of thousands of years that lodes were being broken up and deposited in streams, the topography of the entire area was constantly changing. Massive landslides and titanic upheavals frequently dammed up rivers and streams, forcing the water to find alternate routes. When this happened, the former stream beds were left high and dry, and these often contained much concentrated gold, as can be attested by the following example.

During the Cariboo gold rush, two strolling Chinese miners discovered a large area of gold-bearing land just north of Quesnel. China Cut, as the discovery was named, is estimated to have produced nearly $1,000,000. The discovery was made along the course taken by the Fraser River during the Tertiary era, 70,000,000 to 3,000,000 years ago, and high above the present level. China Cut and the Tertiary Mine, nine miles north of Quesnel, are the only two places yet discovered where the present Fraser River cuts through the ancient Tertiary river bed.

So, always be on the lookout for signs of an ancient or dried-up stream bed, as it could produce gold beyond your wildest dreams. In fact, if a major new placer discovery were to be found today, it undoubtedly would occur in an ancient, un-mined stream bed.

After familiarizing yourself with these six fundamental rules you should have a fairly good working knowledge of what happens to gold once it reaches a stream, giving you a distinct advantage over people who do not have the foggiest notion as to where to start looking. In summary: You know that, once gold enters a stream, it has a tendency to sink to the bottom, eventually making its way to bedrock. However, you also realize that this procedure is dependent upon two important factors; the weight of the nugget and the velocity of the water. In other words, the lighter the gold particle and the more powerful the current, the easier it is for the water to suspend and carry it downstream. On the other hand, the heavier the nugget and the weaker the velocity, the sooner the gold will sink to the bottom.

For the sake of explanation, let us say that the weight of the nuggets and water velocity were such that the gold was being "floated" downstream from its original source. Theoretically then, if a stream were straight, of equal depth and width, free of obstructions, and its downward slope remained constant, prospecting would be futile, since the gold would remained suspended until it reached the ocean. Fortunately, this is not the case. A stream wanders around corners, over, under and around obstructions, forms eddies and whirlpools, drops over waterfalls, and changes velocity constantly.

For a moment, visualize a cork floating downstream. Watch as it is carried over the waterfall and plunges, temporarily, beneath the surface. Then it bobs to the surface and continues downstream until grabbed by the whirling motion of a suction eddy. Eventually freeing itself, the cork continues its journey until its path is blocked by a huge boulder. Here, its progress is impeded until the current forces it around the edge. Finally, the cork is trapped where a fallen tree spans the surface of the stream.

Pieces of gold will react in much the same way. However, as they plunge over the waterfall, the heavier pieces will continue to the bottom and will not resurface. Lighter pieces may be carried by the water's velocity to the suction eddy, where the current slows sufficiently to allow some of them to sink. Similarly, any remaining particles that are hindered by an obstruction will not remain suspended in the water as did the cork, but will take advantage of the reduced water-flow and obstruction and settle on the bottom. And whereas the cork would bob indefinitely where trapped by the fallen tree, gold would sink to the bottom.

You must be able to visualize the progress of gold in this manner as it is floated or dragged downstream. You must be able to understand what effects certain changes in the stream will have upon gold — if you are to be successful. Therefore, the six fundamental rules should be memorized so that you will know what happens to gold after it enters a stream.

There are also three important indicators of gold that you should become acquainted with. These are especially helpful if prospecting a stream about which you know absolutely nothing.

☆ ☆ ☆

(1) BLACK SAND. There are two types of black sand: hematite and magnetite. Hematite is about 70 percent iron, is dark red in colour, and will usually slough out of your pan easily. Magnetite is a far better grade of iron, running 75 percent. It is magnetic, of a darker red, and will not slough out of your pan. Both are frequently found with gold.

☆ ☆ ☆

(2) WATER-WORN ROCKS. While rounded gravel or rocks are not in themselves an indication of gold, they do mean that they have been carried a considerable distance. Sharp, angular rocks very seldom contain gold or other valuable minerals, as they have not travelled far, and, therefore, have not had the opportunity to pick up any good deposits of gold.

☆ ☆ ☆

(3) CEMENTED GRAVEL. The feldspar portion of eroded rocks is carried farther downstream, where it usually collects in a flat area. This is usually a slate-blue or rusty-red colour, and eventually becomes clay, forming a false bedrock upon which gold can be deposited. This cemented gravel has been in place for tens of thousands of years, and it is sometimes so firm that you must hammer the chunks to crumble them. These have produced some good finds for panners in recent years, so be particularly watchful for pockets of cemented gravel.

Although uprooted trees are not necessarily good indicators of gold, they most certainly are excellent places to search. A recently uprooted tree could prove to be a real bonanza, especially if it was located on the inside of a curve. The roots, which probably have pulled up some of the stream bed, could produce some good-sized nuggets, as this deposit likely has never been touched. Never overlook such a possibility!

CHAPTER FOUR

The ABC's Of Gold Panning

BEFORE putting that gold pan into the car and starting out for that secluded mountain, you must also be aware of three, almost equally important factors. First, you must know where to look for placer gold in a stream, utilizing the six fundamental guidelines stressed in the preceding chapter. But that part is relatively simple. Now we must recover that gold, by panning, from the stream. Third, you must be able to separate the gold you recover from the black sands and other concentrates which will accumulate in your pan. (This will be discussed in the next chapter.) These three factors are closely interrelated for being an expert on locating placer deposits is useless if you are unable to pan it. And being and expert gold panner will not get you much gold if you cannot separate it from the waste materials. Therefore, chapters 3, 4 and 5 are very important and demand a great deal of attention.

The basic tool for collecting gold, and by far the most popular, is the gold pan. Even the most elaborate prospecting expedition will still find use for a gold pan — if only to determine the presence of gold before sluicing, dredging or hydraulicking. Although no one has established when gold panning, or washing gold from streams, began, it was practised in ancient times and is depicted on Egyptian monuments dating back to 2900 BC.

As far as is known, the Batea, a conical-shaped wooden dish, was the first vessel fashioned for panning gold. It was developed by the early Mayan Indian civilization, and is still in wide-spread use in Central and South America today. Bateas are somewhat larger than a gold pan, ranging from 15 to 24 inches in diameter and six to eight inches deep. They were used for panning diamonds, emeralds and rubies.

Most gold pans in use in North America today are made of heavy-gauge steel, rounded, with a beaded rim for greater strength. Manufac-

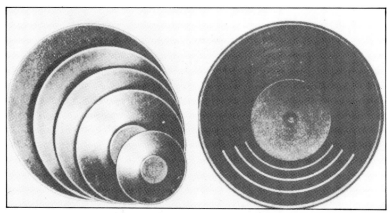

The above photo illustrates a variety of gold pans constructed of heavy gauge steel that range in size from six to 16 inches. Steel pans are heavy and the preservative oil must be burned off before using.

This is a picture of the new, high-impact, plastic gold pan developed with built-in riffles to trap the gold. The plastic pan is lightweight, has a textured surface, and is non-corrosive and acid resistant.

tured by a "spinning" process, these pans are far superior to the crude hand-forged pans that the local blacksmiths used to make. Gold pans come in a range of sizes: six to 10 inches, used primarily for sampling; 12 to 14 inches, often preferred by the novice; and 16 to 18 inches, used by the professionals. The larger pans require greater stamina and technique.

Today, a gold pan moulded from tough, space-age plastic is considered the most efficient pan for the novice. It is superior to the steel pan for several reasons. First, it is rust and corrosive proof. Second, it can be textured with a fine "tooth" to trap the gold better. Third, it is roughly one-quarter the weight of a steel pan. Fourth, it can be tinted a permanent black, thus permitting the tiniest flakes of gold to be easily seen. Its fifth advantage, however, is probably the most important one. Being made of an injection-mould process, riffles can easily be formed into the plastic. These riffles, sometimes called "cheater riffles," trap the gold in much the same way as rifles in a sluice box, thereby not only speeding up the process considerably, but increasing the efficiency as well. These riffles trap much of the gold that the novice might otherwise lose, and greatly increase his gold-panning capability.

If you are using a steel pan, you must first remove all the preservative oil or grease from it, as the oily surface will permit gold to slough out of your pan. This oil can be removed with the application of a strong detergent, or a solvent such as paint thinner. The most common way, however, is to "burn" the pan over the coals of a campfire. Place the pan over the coals until it turns a dull red, then drop it in water. This not only removes the oil, but also gives the pan a dark blue hue, which makes the gold easier to see. If the pan is not a uniform colour,

Three snipers panning for gold at Stout's Gulch near Barkerville in 1938.

repeat the process. Continuing this process will not harm your gold pan, but it could warp if excessive heat is used.

Before you begin panning, you should realize that even an accomplished professional can only process about one cubic yard of material in a 10-hour day. Therefore, if the gravel being panned averages $3 per yard, you are certainly not going to retire on the profits. A six-inch dredge, on the other hand, is capable of processing 20 cubic yards of material ($60) per hour, or $600 for the same 10-hour day. The gold pan, therefore, is generally for recreation or testing for gold. The serious prospector should refer to *Methods of Placer Mining* for ways of processing greater amounts of gold-bearing material in much faster time.

Volume — or the lack of it — therefore, is your biggest drawback when using a gold pan. That's why I cannot overemphasize the fact that you should ignore sandbars while panning. Instead, concentrate your efforts on sniping or crevicing. These terms both mean essentially the same thing — the careful searching and cleaning-out of bedrock cracks and irregularities. These trap particles of gold much like the riffles of a sluice box and are often incredibly rich. The values found at bedrock are often many times those found on the surface, making it well worth the effort of shovelling away the overburden. This is attested to by an experience enjoyed by J.C. Bryant during the Cariboo gold rush. One day during clean-up, he chanced to dig up a piece of bedrock. "It was soft and came off like cheese with the shovel," he later wrote. Just beneath it, "in a hole not much bigger than a gold pan, I saw what I took to be solid gold. I obtained a pan, cleaned it out, then washed what I took out. There were 96 ounces, or a total of $1,543. This was the largest pan of dirt ever taken out of the Cariboo." Today, that same pan of gold would be worth over $40,000.

Once you have reached bedrock, be patient and observe with care. Cover the area slowly, because these places will not be big. Keep it firmly in your mind that a bedrock crack, barely ¼ inch wide by two feet long, can easily trap several hundred dollars' worth of gold.

By now you are probably bubbling with enthusiasm and eager to get started. But before you do, you should look for a place where you can sit and pan comfortably. The water at this point should be at least six inches deep, and flowing just fast enough to keep the muddy water from obscuring your view.

Now, without further ado, let's get to the basics of gold panning itself. Panning is a very simple process, and with a little practice, anyone can pan proficiently. Panning is basically the shaking of heavier materials to the bottom, then washing off the lighter particles from the top. The skilful use of the gold pan could lead to some valuable deposits. If you follow the ABC's of panning listed below.

☆　☆　☆

A — WASHING OFF LARGER ROCKS AND MOSS

(1) Fill your pan about three-quarters full with gold-bearing material

After filling the pan with gold bearing gravel, the author finds a comfortable place to sit where the water is not too swift.

and carry it to the spot you have chosen to do your panning. Submerge the pan deep enough so that it is just under the surface of the water. Now give the pan several vigorous shakes back and forth and from side to side — but not so vigorously as to slough material out of the pan.

(2) Change from the vigorous shaking motion to a gentle circular motion, so that the material starts rotating in a circle. This process will cause most of the dirt to dissolve and wash out of the pan. If roots, moss or lumps of clay occur, break up these lumps by hand while still submerged in the pan.

(3) Scoop out the larger rockers and discard them, after making sure that they are clean.

(4) Repeat processes 1 and 2 to get the smaller rocks to the surface, thereby allowing the heavier material to work its way to the bottom.

☆   ☆   ☆

B — WASHING OFF LIGHTER SAND AND GRAVEL

(1) Hold the pan just below the water and tilted slightly away from the body. Begin rotating the material from side to side, with a slight forward, tossing motion. This must be done carefully, so as not to wash out any of the gold, but with sufficient force to slough the surface and lighter gravel out over the lip of the pan.

(2) Level the pan occasionally, and shake it back and forth and from side to side. This will allow the gold to settle on the bottom, while the lighter material comes to the surface. Repeat process 1 and 2 of step B, increasing the slope of the pan gradually as the material decreases, until only about two cups of heavier material remains in your pan. This material should be composed of black sands, concentrates and — hopefully — gold.

☆　☆　☆

C — WASHING OFF BLACK SANDS AND CONCENTRATES

(1) At this point, lift the pan completely out of the creek, retaining about an inch of water in the pan. Hold the pan in a horizontal position and swirl the mixture gently and slowly in a circular motion. This spreads the material evenly over the bottom of the pan, allowing you to check for nuggets and particles of gold that can easily be picked up by hand or with tweezers.

(2) Once you have done this, submerge the pan again and repeat process 1 and 2 of step B for final concentration. As this is the most critical part of panning, make certain it is accomplished with as much diligence as possible so as not to lose any of the gold. Once you have mastered gold panning, you should be able to continue this procedure until only four or five tablespoons of concentrates are left in your pan. Check the residue for any flakes or grains that can be picked out by tweezers. Do not attempt to pick out all the little specks of fine gold you may see, or you may never get to process your second pan!

The nuggets, grains or flakes you have recovered should be placed in a plastic container. An empty pill bottle with a screw top will serve the purpose nicely. Then dump the remainder of your concentrates into a large bucket for later processing. Once you know that you are recovering gold, your next priority is to accumulate as much concentrates as you can in a working day. Do not waste time trying to separate fine gold from the black sands after every pan. Instead, dump your concentrates into a bucket, and process the entire lot later on. This will allow you to handle more gravel, recover and process more gold, and thereby increase your efficiency — and return.

When using a gold pan, ignore the minute specks of glittering yellow known as "flour" gold. You are only wasting your time and effort. One small piece of gold no larger than a grain of rice contains more gold, by weight, then all the flour gold you can accumulate in a full day's hard panning. However, flour gold is a good indication of gold in the area. It also indicates it has travelled a considerable distance from its original source. Therefore, when you find flour, or fine, gold, move

GOLD PANNING TECHNIQUES

(A) After filling pan ¾ full of material, submerge it in water. Then knead it as with bread dough, allowing gold to settle on the bottom.

(B) Remove any rocks or large pieces of material and discard.

(C) Give the pan several vigourous shakes back and forth and from side to side, or hit the pan sharply with the open hand. This will help to move the heavier concentrates to the bottom.

(D) Hold the pan just below the water and tilted slightly from the body. Begin rotating the pan from side to side, allowing the lighter sand to be flushed over the lip.

(E) Level the pan occasionally, shake it back and forth, checking for nuggets. Then continue the panning procedure until nothing remains in your pan but black sand and concentrates. These should be stored for later processing.

farther upstream and try again. Remember, gold particles will continually increase in size as you approach the source where they first entered the stream.

If you are unable to find any traces of "colour," then abandon that spot and try again farther upstream. But watch for other promising signs in your pan. For example, black sands, or particles that are red, green, pink, transparent or metallic in colour, indicate that you are in an area of mineralization. Some pyrites thought to be iron could be platinum, nickel, ruthenium, cobalt, copper, or even gold and silver. Some of the tiny black, brown, white or red particles that compose your concentrates could be columbite, tantalite, cobalt or a few others. Some of the early prospectors used mercury in their recovery work, and lost large quantities of it in streams over the years. Mercury will amalgamate with gold, forming small greyish balls. In the Granite Creek area of British Columbia, platinum was recovered by the old-timers, along with the gold. The Amur River in Russia is the only other river in the world where gold and platinum are known to have been recovered side by side. The prospectors in the Similkameen region considered the silvery-white metal worthless, however, and for a while they discarded it. So, never throw away any suspicious looking concentrates until you can determine its value.

CHAPTER FIVE

How To Recover Fine Gold

F OR the sake of argument, let us assume that the first area you begin panning produces worthwhile quantities of gold. Your next step, therefore, is to recover as much of the precious metal as possible in a working day. This is best accomplished by panning down to the heavier concentrates and dumping this residue in a large bucket. At the end of the day you should have accumulated a quantity of fine gold, a few flakes and, perhaps, even a small nugget or two. But these are still mixed in with black sand and other concentrates, and you must now separate the gold. There are a number of ways this can be accomplished.

☆ ☆ ☆

MAGNET

Before using a magnet, the concentrates must be thoroughly dried. If you are using a plastic pan, apply the magnet underneath the pan and move it in a circular motion with the pan slightly tilted. The magnet will attract the black sand, leaving the gold isolated. If you are using a steel pan, or a lot of concentrates at one time, wrap the magnet is a thin sheet of cellophane. Then pass the magnet over the concentrates. When the magnet is covered with black sand, remove the wrapping. This will allow the waste particles to drop freely to the ground and keep your magnet clean. Then repeat the process until you have recovered all the magnetic particles from the concentrates. A magnet will only recover magnetite, leaving hematite and other non-magnetic particles in the pan with the gold. The magnet's inability to recover all unwanted particles from the concentrates makes this system inefficient, as best.

☆ ☆ ☆

FLOTATION PROCESS

In the flotation process, the concentrate is mixed with water, chemical conditioning reagents, and collecting reagents. When air is passed

Fig. 3
THE CYANIDE PROCESS
FROM TONS OF ORE, A BUTTON OF GOLD BULLION

1. Tons of gold-bearing ore must be processed to produce one ounce of gold.

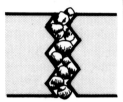

2. Steel jaws shatter ore into softball-size fragments. Hand sorters discard pieces lacking gold.

3. After further crushing, the ore mixes with water and enters a revolving cyclinder, to be pulverized by tumbling steel balls or bars.

4. Air jets and mechanical arms in agitator tanks mix cyanide into powdered ore and water, called slime. This releases gold from rock.

5. The gold-cyanide solution and slime funnel into vast tanks where the rock particles slowly sink. The clarified solution is fed into filtration units.

6. Gold-cyanide solution is filtered to strain out any remaining rock particles and then is deaerated.

7. Zinc dust added to the solution separates the cyanide from the gold, which emerges as an impure powder.

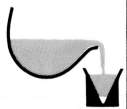

8. The gold is melted with fluxes such as borax. As the metal cools in the bottom of a conical mold, the fluxes combine with impurities and float as slag.

9. Final product: a shining "button" 90 percent gold, the rest silver. Further processing at a central refinery yields the 99.6% pure gold.

through the mixture, mineral particles cling to the bubbles which rises to form a froth on the surface. The waste material (gangue) settles to the bottom. The froth is then skimmed off and distilled or otherwise removed, leaving a clean concentrate. This method is also called the froth-flotation process.

☆ ☆ ☆

CYANIDE PROCESS

In this process the concentrate is placed in a tank containing a weak solution of cyanide. Gold dissolves in a sodium-cyanide solution, when air or oxygen is present, to form a compound of sodium, gold and cyanide. From this substance the precious metal is precipitated by the action of another metal, such as zinc. Mills have largely adopted this method over the amalgamation process. (See Fig. 3.)

☆ ☆ ☆

AMALGAMATION

The amalgamation process is one of the oldest and simplest methods of recovering fine gold. The process employs the use of mercury, a soft liquid-metal, which has a tendency to assimilate heavier metals like gold or platinum, while ignoring the lighter sands and gravels. The crushed ore, or concentrates, are treated with the mercury, forming an alloy called amalgam. Amalgams are made in many different ways, by using sluices, riffle tables, mechanical amalgamators, jigs, or just a plain gold pan.

Before gold can be amalgamated, however, it must first be cleaned of iron rust and impurities. These impurities not only make gold difficult to amalgamate and to identify, but can also cause you to lose more than 25 percent of the rust-coated gold.

Two gold "buttons" recovered by the Cyanide Process. These came from the Mosquito Creek mine in the Cariboo in 1972.

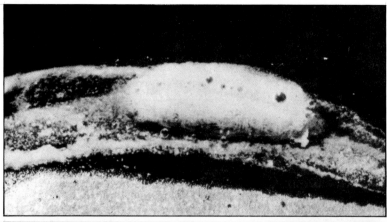

(Top) As mercury becomes contaminated, it will break apart into tiny droplets, making proper amalgamation impossible. When this happens, the mercury can be cleaned with a diluted solution of nitric acid.
(Above) The clean mercury will form a "ball"

The simplest method of cleaning gold is by using nitric acid. First, dump your concentrates in a plastic gold pan, or some other container that will not be affected by the powerful acid. Cover the concentrates with about one-half inch of water, then add a small amount of nitric acid. When the water-to-acid ratio reaches 30 to one, the solution will begin to boil. Once boiling starts, swirl the mixture around gently — taking care not to splash yourself (good rubber gloves would be an asset here) in the process — making sure all the material has been exposed. Then rinse away the acid solution by dunking your pan in the stream. Upon pouring off the excess water, your concentrates should be ready for amalgamation.

First, add about one-half teaspoon of mercury to five pounds of concentrates, then place underwater and agitate. The mercury should be worked thoroughly through the concentrates for complete contact with all gold. The gold will then be assimilated by the mercury, giving it a pasty consistency. The mercury will appear rough on the outside of the "ball" after it has gathered the gold.

Panning in the usual manner will wash off the waste sands, but care must be taken so as not to lose any of the tiny drops of mercury which will gradually unite into a single mass.

All the gold that was contained within the black sands and other

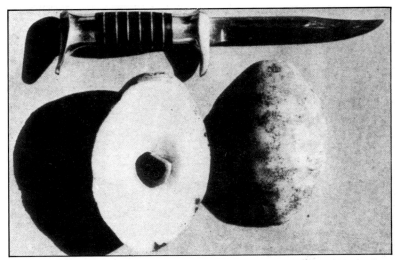

One of the simplest ways of separating an amalgam of gold and mercury is to retort it in an ordinary potato.

concentrates is now trapped in the ball of mercury, and there are a number of ways of separating the two. Remember that mercury is expensive, so it is wise to recover as much as possible for future use. One way of doing this is to place the amalgam in a buckskin, chamois skin, or some other tightly-woven fabric such as canvas. Then squeeze out as much mercury as possible. This should be done underwater, as mercury tends to splatter otherwise. The remaining mercury is then "burned" off, leaving pure gold. **WARNING:** Extreme caution must be exercised when heating mercury, as the fumes are deadly.

The "Baked Potato Method" is a popular, simple way of separating the gold and mercury, which can be done almost anywhere. First, cut a large potato in half, then scoop out a small depression in one of the halves with a spoon or knife. The amalgam is then placed into this cavity, and the two halves are re-united and wired together. The potato is then wrapped in several layers of aluminum foil, to prevent the loss of mercury vapours, and placed in a campfire to bake. After about 45 minutes, depending upon the size of the potato and amalgam, the mercury will have vaporizer and saturated the potato, leaving pure gold in the cavity. After removing the gold, crush the potato and pan the mercury in the usual manner. But do not eat the potato!

The "Mercury Retort" is by far the most common way of freeing gold from the amalgam. A retort can be extremely dangerous if handled carelessly, or so simple that a child could operate it. The retort is a mechanical device used for separating the gold and mercury, while retaining the mercury for future use. It consists simply of a cast iron pot with a tight-fitting lid, which is connected to a condenser which actually does the work of recovering the mercury. (See Fig. 4.)

The amalgam is placed inside the bowl (A), which should first be

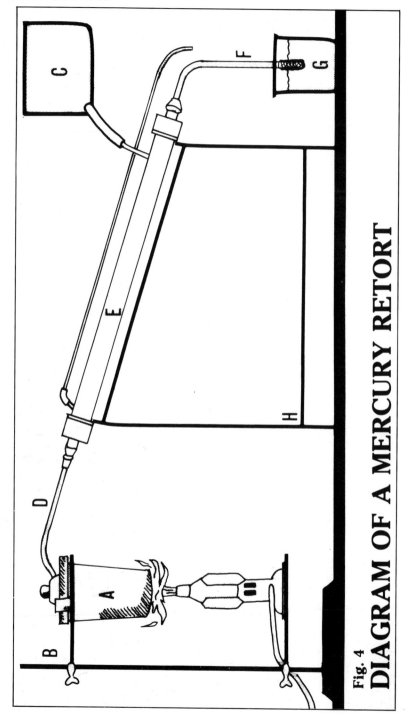

Fig. 4
DIAGRAM OF A MERCURY RETORT

(Above) A prospector squeezing an amalgam of gold and mercury from a cleanup on the Fraser River, five miles north of Quesnel, B.C., in 1938. The amalgam is squeezed through a chamois, permitting the mercury to seep through into the pan where it is collected for future use.

(Below) An amalgam from which most of the mercury has been squeezed out. This amalgam ball is then heated, usually in a retort, to burn off the remaining mercury, leaving almost pure gold.

coated with a film of chalk so as to prevent the gold and silver from adhering to its cast iron sides. The bowl, up to two-thirds full, is then sealed and clamped shut. The lid should be luted with a flour paste or an asbestos paste-ring, and must be airtight to prevent the escape of deadly mercury vapours. By blowing hard into the condenser tube, you will be able to tell if air is escaping. If the lid is leaking, remove it and re-lute, and test again. This is a very important aspect of your operation — your life could depend on it.

Next, place the retort bowl, with the condenser attached, into the clamp (B), and fill the tank (C) full of water with the pipelines in the proper position. Remove the water tank lid and leave off while firing. Place the propane torch about one-half inch from the bowl and, starting with a low flame, gradually increase the heat after a few minutes. At around 675 degrees Fahrenheit the mercury will vaporize and escape through the tube (D) to the condenser (E). The condenser, which is simply a water-jacket wrapped around the tube, cools the mercury as it passes and converts it back into a liquid form. Continue applying heat until the mercury stops coming from the condenser pipe (F). The receptacle (G) should contain water so as to prevent the mercury from splattering.

The time required for this operation, depending upon the amount of amalgam placed in the bowl, varies from 30 minutes to two hours. Once the mercury has completely vaporized, the pot is allowed to cool for at least 30 minutes, when the lid is removed. CAUTION — as the retort cools, it will create a suction and draw water back into the hot bowl. This could cause an explosion, so always remove the condenser pipe from the water tank anytime heat is not being applied.

If some mercury remains in the condenser pipe it can be saved by standing the free end of the condenser in the container of water, and tapping it lightly with a stick. Flushing the tube with water will remove any traces of mercury that remain and clean the tube for the next time.

The same mercury can be used over and over again, but as dirt begins to accumulate, the mercury will discolour and crumble into many small particles, preventing complete amalgamation. When this occurs, a 30 to one solution of water to nitric acid will clean the dirt from the mercury and it will be as clean as before.

Recovering gold through amalgamation will save an incredible amount of fine gold that might otherwise have been lost. But regardless of what system you use to separate the gold from the amalgam, always remember that mercury vapours are deadly, so never inhale them. As a precautionary measure, always stand upwind when heating mercury.

Chapter Six

Equipment

REGARDLESS whether you are an experienced professional, or an amateur weekend prospector, there are a certain number of items that should be included in your equipment. Some of the more important items are listed below, although they are not all essential, depending upon how serious or thorough a job you intend doing. Likewise, this is not a complete list. You may want to add items that will make your job easier and faster, and your stay more comfortable. This will vary with the individual, depending upon: (1) how far you have to backpack your equipment; (2) the area you are prospecting; (3) the type of work you plan to do, and; (4) how long you plan to stay. For example, if you were planning on spending two weeks at the site, you would require a tent, bedding and a large quantity of food that would not be needed for a one-day excursion. Therefore, on a one-day trip you would be able to pack much more needed equipment than you could when carrying a two weeks' supply of food. In this case, it might be wise to make two trips to the site, thus making sure that you have all the food and other supplies you will require for your extended stay.

THE GOLD PAN. An absolute must for all prospectors, regardless if you will be using a rocker or building a sluice box at the site. Gold pans can be obtained at most hardware stores in Canada or the United States — provided they are not sold out. The plastic gold pan is recommended for the novice; however, if you are unable to obtain one, purchase the steel variety. Remember to burn off the preservative oil before using a steel pan. If you are unable to locate a gold pan, a non-enamelled frying pan, some cooking pots or a wash basin will make adequate substitutes.

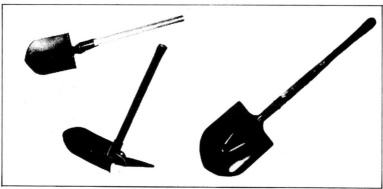

SHOVEL. Whether you use a short, or long-handled shovel depends greatly upon the type of work it will be used for. Shovels with shorter handles are lighter, easier to manage and carry on long trips, and are suitable for crevicing, or pot-holing. However, if you plan to do a lot of shovelling, such as loading a Tom or sluice, your best bet is to get a shovel with a long handle. You can work faster and the long handle makes shovelling much easier on the back. Whatever type you decide upon, make certain that it is sturdily constructed and has a rounded point, as you will invariable be using it to move large objects or obstructions (a square-mouthed shovel is virtually worthless for digging). Holes drilled into the shovel will allow the water to drain quickly, thereby reducing some of the weight.

PICK. The standard miner's pick is your best bet for prospecting. It is strong, but light-weight, and very efficient. A miner's pick will prove indispensable if you encounter tough clay or cemented-gravel. The points can also be wedged in bedrock cracks, allowing easier access to the gold.

A geologist's pick may come in handy as well, especially for breaking off pieces of suspicious looking rock you may find. The flat end is also useful for breaking up chunks of tough clay before washing.

AXE. Like the shovel, the type of axe you use depends upon your individual needs. A small single-bitted hatchet is sufficient for cutting firewood or driving tent pegs. But if you plan on travelling seldom used back roads, a large single-bitted axe is recommended, as a hatchet would be virtually useless in cutting through large fallen trees that might block your path. Some people carry both axes in the car, but carry only the hatchet to the campsite.

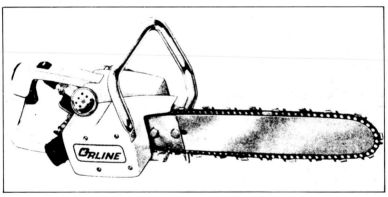

CHAIN SAW. One of the most powerful tools in the bush these days is the small gasoline-powered chain saw. Lightweight and dependable, it can be an indispensable tool in the bush, particularly for removing windfalls which obstruct many seldom used back roads.

PRY BAR. A pry bar or crow bar is a necessary and very useful tool used in crevicing and the widening of bedrock cracks. It is also helpful in getting leverage to move heavy objects. And the points of a pry bar are excellent for breaking up clay or cemented-gravel.

TWEEZERS. A necessity to aid in the recovery of small grains of gold from the concentrates that are easily spotted, but difficult to remove with stubby fingers. A pointed pair is preferred, but blunt ones work just as well.

☆　☆　☆

BRUSHES. For the cleaning-out of bedrock cracks and crevices, a variety of brushes are an absolute must. A small whisk broom will easily get the coarser material, while a small, fine-haired paint brush (about 1 inch) will sweep out the finer particles. As gold usually concentrates in bedrock cracks, it is imperative that these be thoroughly cleaned out, and small brushes are best for this purpose.

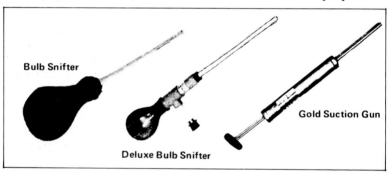

Bulb Snifter

Gold Suction Gun

Deluxe Bulb Snifter

CREVICING GUN. (Also called a gold sniffer.) This tool is vital to your operation if you are cleaning out crevices that are underwater. The crevicing gun is simply a grease, or caulking gun, with a long tube attached into one end. Pulling out on the handle creates a vacuum that sucks in the water-gravel mixture. Pushing the handle expels the water, but retains the gold-bearing sand for later panning. The gold sniffer replaces a rubber bulb for the crevicing-gun's handle, but the principles are the same.

GOLD BOTTLE. A necessary item for storing the fine gold and nuggets you recover. These are much more practical that the "gold pokes" used by prospectors of old. The common pill bottle will serve this purpose nicely. Plastic containers with screw lids are preferred, as there is less chance of breakage or of the cap falling off. If you keep your bottle topped up with water, it will prevent you from losing some of the finer gold each time the top is removed.

☆　☆　☆

CANVAS BAG. A large canvas bag is required for storing your black sands and concentrates prior to final separation. A plain bucket or pail is equally efficient, but an empty canvas bag is much easier to carry to the site.

☆　☆　☆

MAGNET. Useful for cleaning the magnetite from concentrates before amalgamation. (Some fine cellophane is a handy accessory.)

MERCURY. If you plan to recover fine gold from your concentrates at the site, a small vial of mercury, a few potatoes, and some aluminium foil are about all you will need. As a small amount of mercury can literally recover pounds of gold, unless it is burned off, about three or four ounces is all that is required. Always remember to be careful when applying heat to mercury.

☆　☆　☆

STEEL TEASPOONS. Steel teaspoons and tablespoons are excellent for cleaning out small cracks and crevices which are too small for a shovel. A sturdy garden trowel is also handy for these hard-to-get-at-places.

☆　☆　☆

OPTIONAL EQUIPMENT

Below is a list of a number of items which could be considered optional, again, depending upon the varied needs of the individual and the locality. Generally speaking, this equipment is geared more towards the comfort and safety of the prospector, than to the act of prospecting itself.

☆　☆　☆

MAP AND COMPASS. Before entering the forest, learn to read your map and compass, especially if you are entering unfamiliar territory, or venturing some distance off the main road. Government topographical maps are recommended, for, in addition to showing streams and roads, they also describe the contour of the land. Topographical maps are rendered in great detail, cover small or large areas, and can be purchased from the government or through your local map dealer at nominal cost and are a cheap, but worthwhile investment. When using a compass in coastal British Columbia, remember it reads about 22 degrees east of true north.

☆　☆　☆

CANTEEN. If you will be prospecting in a particularly hot or dry region, or you are uncertain as to whether you will find fresh water in the area, it is wise to take along a canteen of water. If you do find water, boiling it is the best way to purify it. If it tastes flat, add a few pieces of charcoal from the fire to sweeten it. Never drink water from a pond, stream or lake in which no aquatic life is visible, as this is a sign of natural poisoning. Dead animals along the shore is another.

☆　☆　☆

MATCHES. Matches are a must on all excursions into the woods, and they should be carried in a waterproof container. These containers can be purchased at most sporting goods stores. If you are unable to obtain one, wrap your matches in tinfoil or some other waterproof material, then place them in a small bottle with a tight-fitting lid. Take special care to keep your matches dry, as wet matches are useless. When extinguishing your fire, do it properly. Pour water on it, then stir the ashes. Do this three times. If it is still smoking or steaming, repeat the process. Remember, a smouldering fire can ignite several days later and cause a forest fire — so make certain your fire is dead out!

☆　☆　☆

KNIFE. A good hunting knife is recommended. It can be carried on your belt at little or no inconvenience, and will come in handy when preparing food, or when cutting a potato in preparation for amalgamation. If you do not have a hunting knife, a sturdy jackknife will make an excellent substitute. (NOTE: Always tie pieces of bright red yarn to small valuable items such as car keys, compass, knife, etc. This way, if you misplace them, you stand a far better chance of finding them.)

☆　☆　☆

BOOTS. Wear the best boots you can afford that are well-made, but not too heavy. They should be broken in before you set out. Take along extra socks and laces. Take frequent rest breaks. Remember, your feet and legs are carrying you and your equipment, and they deserve the best of care.

☆　☆　☆

SHEET OF PLASTIC. A lightweight sheet of plastic, when folded, requires very little space, but it could be worth considerably more than its weight in gold if you get caught in a sudden downpour. By draping it over yourself, or by tying it tent style over a branch, you can keep dry and comfortable. The sheet is also useful for collecting rain water for drinking when other water is unavailable. Dew can be collected in this way as well.

☆　☆　☆

FIRST AID KIT. It is always practical to make room for a first aid kit, especially when travelling alone — which is not recommended. Far too many accidents can overtake the unwary prospector, especially one inexperienced in forest travel. As a safety precaution, always give full details of your trip to responsible people such as friends or relatives. Inform the local authorities, conservation officer, or forester of your intentions as well. Equally important, report to them when you come out so that they and others will not risk their lives in an unnecessary search for you.

☆ ☆ ☆

SNAKE BITE KIT. In many regions of the United States, and in some areas of British Columbia, there is a danger of encountering rattlesnakes. For this reason, it is wise to carry along a snake bite kit. In areas frequented by the little critters, it is best to sleep in a tent at night, as they will crawl up and sleep next to anything nice and warm — like a human body!

☆ ☆ ☆

SLEEPING BAG. If you are staying overnight or longer, take along a lightweight sleeping bag. It will help keep you warm and comfortable during those cool mountain nights.

☆ ☆ ☆

HAT. If you plan on prospecting in hot, open areas, you will find a cowboy-style hat, or hat with a wide brim, very cooling, the brim shading your face.

☆ ☆ ☆

METAL DETECTOR. This modern-day marvel can also be used when prospecting for mineral deposits. However, not all models are equipped for prospecting. Because there are so many on the market, you would do best by checking with your local metal detector dealer or by checking the advertising columns of treasure magazines.

☆ ☆ ☆

WHERE TO PURCHASE YOUR EQUIPMENT

Most of the equipment described in this chapter can be obtained from your local hardware store. Specialized gold mining equipment not available in hardware stores can be obtained from companies dealing specifically in that type of equipment. A prospector's catalog can be obtained free of charge by writing to: KEENE ENGINEERING, 9330 Corbin Ave., Northridge, Calif. 91324. In Canada write to: ROCKY MOUNTAIN DETECTORS, Box 5366, Station A, Calgary, Alta. T2H 1X8.

CHAPTER SEVEN

Guide To Staking Claims In British Columbia

O N August 15, 1988, the Mineral Act and the Mining (Placer) Act were repealed. In their places, a new Act known as the Mineral Tenure Act was proclaimed. This new Act consolidates the other two Acts, and outlines the duties and responsibilities of both free miners and administrators. The main objective of the Mineral Tenure Act is to improve administrative procedures, making the process of acquiring and maintaining mineral titles more consistent, streamlined, and up-to-date.

The British Columbia Ministry of Energy, Mines and Petroleum Resources has prepared a 55-page guide to assist would-be prospectors and miners with the new Mineral Tenure Act. Entitled, *George's Guide to Claim Staking in B.C.,* the booklet may be purchased for $1.07 from:

Ministry of Energy, Mines & Petroleum Resources
Mineral Titles Branch
Ste. 302, 865 Hornby St.
Vancouver, B.C.
V6Z 2G3

The highlights of the guide, as it pertains to placer claims, has been excerpted in this chapter.

CONTACT THE GOLD COMMISSIONER

You must contact the appropriate Gold Commissioner before prospecting to get the current mineral titles information on the area in which you intend to work. To find the location of a Gold Commissioner's office, contact the Government Agent listed in the blue pages of the telephone directory. The Gold Commissioner will provide maps, tags, staking regulations, forms, and other information on title acquisition.

FREE MINER CERTIFICATE

Only Free Miners can locate and acquire mineral titles in British

Province of British Columbia
Ministry of Energy, Mines and Petroleum Resources

APPLICATION FOR INDIVIDUAL
FREE MINER CERTIFICATE

Before completing form, please read information on back.

THE FOLLOWING MUST BE COMPLETED FULLY BY THE APPLICANT. FAILURE TO DO SO
WILL CAUSE DELAY IN THE ISSUANCE OF THE FREE MINER CERTIFICATE.

(PLEASE PRINT FULL NAME IN BLOCK LETTERS)

(Surname)

(First Name)

(Second Name)

ISSUING OFFICE ONLY

F.M.C. No. Issued

Permanent F.M.C. Code

Issued at

Date of Issue

Valid from .... to Dec. 31

MAILING ADDRESS ....

(Street/Box No.)

(Province/State)

(City)

(Postal/Zip Code)

(Telephone) ( )

ALL APPLICANTS TO COMPLETE THIS SECTION

Are you over 18 years of age? Yes ☐ No ☐   Are you over 65 years of age? Yes ☐ No ☐

ARE YOU A CANADIAN CITIZEN? Yes ☐ No ☐

If "No", please complete the following questions.

APPLICANTS WHO ARE *NOT* CANADIAN CITIZENS *MUST* COMPLETE THIS SECTION

ARE YOU A LANDED IMMIGRANT? Yes ☐ No ☐
A landed immigrant qualifies as a permanent resident of Canada for the purposes of this application. Proof of status may be requested. (Refer to Section 7 (2) (a) on back)

OR

HAVE YOU HELD A FREE MINER CERTIFICATE EVERY YEAR SINCE JANUARY 1, 1978? ☐ ☐
(Refer to Section 7 (4) (a) on back)

OR

ARE YOU REQUESTING THE ISSUANCE OF A FREE MINER CERTIFICATE, AUTHORIZED BY ORDER OF THE MINISTER? ☐ ☐
ARE YOU REQUESTING THE ISSUANCE OF A FREE MINER CERTIFICATE, AUTHORIZED BY ORDER OF THE MINISTER?
(Refer to Section 7 (4) (b) on back) (A certificate may be granted for one year to facilitate financial and estate transactions involving mineral titles)

NOTE: If yes this application will be forwarded to Victoria, prior to issuance for processing.

I hereby certify that the information given in this application is true and complete in every respect.

(Date)

(Signature)

Columbia. To become a Free Miner you must obtain a Free Miner Certificate. These are available to:

1. Any Canadian citizen or permanent resident who is 18 years of age or over;

2. Canadian corporations;

3. Partnerships of those qualifying under 1 or 2 above.

You can apply for a Free Miner Certificate at the office of any Gold Commissioner or Sub-Recorder in the province.

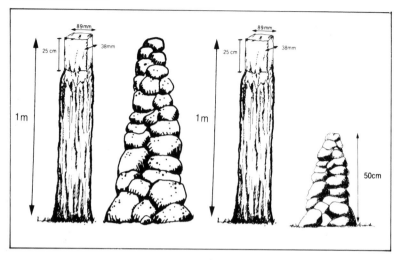

METAL CLAIM-STAKING TAGS

In order to stake a valid claim you must purchase the appropriate metal tags which are available at all Gold Commissioners' and Sub-Recorders' offices. These metal tags must be firmly attached to the posts with four broad-headed nails, one at each corner of the tag.

POSTS

Posts are used to establish the location of all claims. These posts must meet certain minimum specifications. There are two types of posts: legal posts and identification posts. Legal and identification posts can be made of either a piece of sound timber, a stump or tree cut to the same specifications as a post, or a cairn of rocks.

If you use a wooden post or tree, it must meet the following size specifications:

1. It must be at least one metre (39.37 inches) above the ground in height.

2. It must be squared and faced on four sides for at least 25 centimetres (9.8 inches) from the top.

3. The dimensions of the top of the post must be at least:

    i. 89mm x 89mm (3½in x 3½in) for legal posts

    ii. 38mm x 89 mm (1½in x 3½in) for identification posts.

If you use a cairn of stones it must stand at least:

1. 1 metre (39.37 inches) in height for legal posts

2. 50 centimetres (19.69 inches) in height for identification posts.

Posts and cairns must be placed securely in the ground. If you use improper posts or cairns, or do not place them securely, your claims may be invalid.

PLACER CLAIMS

Placer claims can only be located in those areas designated as Placer Claim Lands or Placer Lease Lands. The location of Placer Claim Lands and Placer Lease Lands is shown on Placer Titles Reference Maps. Note that within a larger area that is "open" to placer

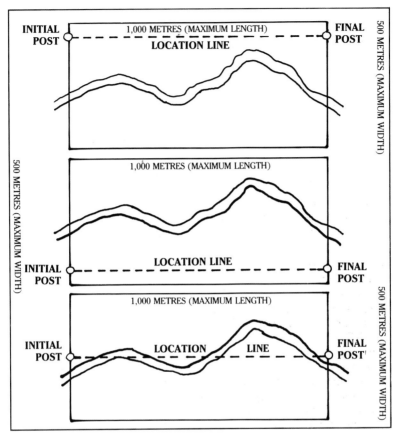

activity there may be several smaller reserves where staking is prohibited.

There is no limit to the number of placer claims a Free Miner may stake per year.

SIZE AND SHAPE OF PLACER CLAIMS

The maximum size of a placer claim is 500 metres by 1,000 metres. The position of a placer claim is defined by placing one post at each end of a "location line." The length of the claim is measured along the location line and cannot be more than 1,000 metres. *The location line cannot change direction.*

The width of a placer claim is measured at right angles to the location line. The maximum width is 500 metres, which can be measured entirely to the left of the location line, entirely to the right of the location line, or some on the left and some on the right of the location line.

(NOTE: *The left and right sides of a location line are determined by standing on the location line, with your back to the initial post (No. 1), and facing the final post (No. 2). The left and right banks of a stream are determined by facing downstream.*)

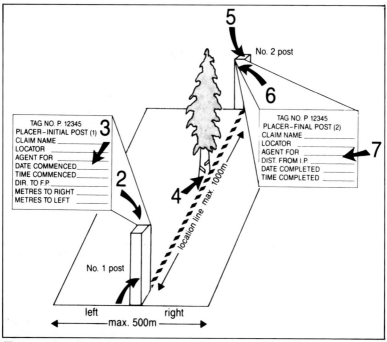

TAG NO. P. 12345
PLACER–INITIAL POST (1) **3**
CLAIM NAME _____
LOCATOR _____
AGENT FOR _____
DATE COMMENCED_____
TIME COMMENCED_____
DIR. TO F.P._____
METRES TO RIGHT _____
METRES TO LEFT _____

TAG NO. P. 12345
PLACER–FINAL POST (2)
CLAIM NAME _____
LOCATOR _____
AGENT FOR _____
DIST. FROM I.P. _____
DATE COMPLETED _____
TIME COMPLETED _____

5

No. 2 post

6

7

2

4

location line max. 1000m

No. 1 post

left   right
—max. 500m—

The procedure for staking a placer claim. The numbers 1 to 7 correspond to the steps outlined in the text below.

PROCEDURE FOR STAKING A PLACER CLAIM

1. Place a legal post at one end of the proposed location line. This becomes the "No. 1 post."

2. Firmly affix to this post on the side facing the location line, the top half of a metal tag issued for placer claims and embossed with the words "PLACER INITIAL POST (NO. 1)."

3. Mark the metal tag with the required information.

4. Mark the location line by blazing trees on two sides facing the line, and by cutting underbrush. Flagging, paint, and picket lines may be used in addition. *On private property, contact the owner before blazing or cutting trees.*

5. Place another legal post at the other end of the location line, not more than 1,000 metres from the No. 1 post. This post becomes the "No. 2 post."

6. Firmly affix to this post, on the side facing the No. 1 post, the bottom half of the metal tag embossed with the words "PLACER FINAL POST (NO. 2)."

7. Mark the metal tag with the required information.

If a cairn of rocks is used as either post, the metal tag must be placed securely inside the cairn.

The location is complete when the No. 1 and No. 2 posts have been placed, the location line marked, and the required information marked

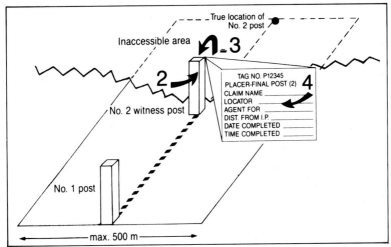

The procedure for staking a placer claim using a witness post. The numbers 2 to 4 correspond to the text below.

on the tags in this manner.

WITNESS POST FOR PLACER CLAIMS

Under some circumstances it may be impossible to place a final post in the correct location because of the presence of water, ice, or due to topographical conditions. In this case you may use a "witness post" for the No. 2 post. A witness post cannot be used for the No. 1 post. A witness post must be placed according to the following procedure which is illustrated in the figure below.

1. Follow steps 1 to 4 in the procedure for locating a placer claim, which include: placing the No. 1 post; affixing the metal tag; marking the required information; and marking the location line.

2. Place a legal post on the location line as close as possible to where the No. 2 post should be. This becomes the witness post.

3. Mark this post on the side facing away from the No. 1 post with:

    i. The words "NO. 2 WITNESS POST"

    ii. The true bearing and distance to the point where the No. 2 post should be.

4. Firmly affix to the same side as above a metal tag, issued for placer claims, and embossed with the words "PLACER FINAL POST (NO. 2)," and fill in the required information.

AFTER LOCATING A CLAIM

Placer claims acquire title as soon as staking is completed. However, an application to record any claim must be made within 20 days after the location is completed. To record your placer claim, apply at the Gold Commissioner's office, or a Sub-Recorder's office, for the mining division in which the claim is located. You may send the application to the appropriate office by mail; however, it must be received before the expiry of the 20 day period.

The application must include a completed application form, a sketch plan and the prescribed fee. The application form requires a statement accurately describing access to the claim. It must describe, in relation to topographical features, cultural features, roads, buildings, etc., the location of the No. 1 post of a placer claim. The sketch map must be accurate since it will be used to update the title maps. Clearly indicate the boundaries of the claim and the position of the applicable legal posts on a page-size portion of a Placer Titles Reference Map.

CHAPTER EIGHT

Prospector's Dictionary

O N the following pages you will find a glossary of mining terminology popular with old prospectors and modern miners. Many are taken from context, but are repeated in abbreviated form for quick reference as to meaning. This is by no means a comprehensive dictionary of all mining terms, phrases, minerals or equipment, but it should be sufficient to give the novice a working knowledge.

☆ ☆ ☆

ADIT. A horizontal or inclined entrance into a mine.

ALCHEMY. The forerunner of modern chemistry. Its chief aims were the transmuting of base metals into gold, and the discovery of an elixir of life.

ALLOY. When two or more metals are melted or joined together, an alloy is formed. This is done to harden or strengthen other metals, such as silver added to gold; or to form a metal not found in nature: e.g., copper and zinc to form brass. Alloys have different properties from their constituent elements: e.g., they are poorer conductors of heat and electricity, often harder, and with the exception of aluminum alloys, more resistant to corrosion.

ALLUVIAL MINING. The practice of working a natural alluvial fan where centuries of erosion has washed down great mountains into wide, sloping deposits of loosely packed dirt, stones, gravel and boulders. (See also Deposits.)

AMALGAMATION. This is a mining

term relating to the combination of metal such as silver, platinum or gold, with mercury. Amalgamation is one of the simplest and easiest ways of recovering fine gold from concentrates.

ANALYSIS. See **Assay.**

ANCIENT STREAM BED. Due to landslides, earth tremors and other natural forces, the course of a river was often dammed and forced to seek alternate routes. These "old channels," or ancient river beds are eagerly sought by prospectors, as their gold-bearing gravels have never been touched.

ANNEAL. The process of heating, then cooling slowly, for the purpose of making metals less brittle.

APRON. In a rocker, this refers to the burlap or canvas that is stretched across the frame, at an incline, beneath the hopper. It traps the fine particles of gold as they fall through the perforated holes of the hopper's bottom.

AQUA REGIA. A mixture containing one part nitric acid to four parts hydrochloric acid which is strong enough to dissolve gold and platinum.

ASSAY. The evaluation or analysis of ore to determine the proportion of gold, silver or other valuable metals. Usually an assay is done by chemical methods and is fairly accurate.

ASSIMILATE. This is the ability of mercury to absorb gold, silver or platinum into a common ball, or alloy, called amalgam, while ignoring lighter sands and gravel.

AURIFEROUS QUARTZ MINING.

These are mines where gold is produced as the main metal, not a by-product.

AVOIRDUPOIS WEIGHT. This refers to the common English and American system of weight measure. This system is not used for medicine, gold or other precious metals.

437½ grains . . . . 1 ounce
7,000 grains . . . . 16 ounces
16 ounces . . . . 1 pound

BAKED POTATO METHOD. A method of separating gold from the amalgam.

BAR. This term was given to submerged sandbars that formed in a creek or river. It increased in size as dirt, sand, gravel, black sands and gold were deposited. Sandbars have produced great quantities of gold in the past and should not be overlooked today, if you employ equipment which can process the gold-bearing gravels rapidly.

BARREN. An area of a river or stream that is incapable of producing gold, produces very little, or has been completely mined out.

BASE-METAL MINING. This is the mining of metals such as cop-

Cleaning bedrock on Stout's Gulch, near Barkerville.

per, lead, zinc, tin, aluminum, etc., as opposed to precious metals such as silver, gold or platinum.

BATTERY. Another name for a stamp mill.

BEDROCK. Originally, this referred to the solid rock bottom of a stream or river. A false bedrock is formed when the feldspar portion of eroded rocks gathers and settles creating a tough clay or cemented gravel. The largest quantities of gold are generally recovered within a couple of feet above bedrock.

BENCHES. A flat area above a stream or river.

BLACK SAND. Usually composed of hematite and magnetite, black sands are heavier than ordinary sands and settle much in the same manner as does gold. For this reason, black sands are good indicators of gold and should never be overlooked. When panning, black sands will normally comprise most of the concentrates remaining in the pan.

BONANZA. This is a term used to describe an exceptionally rich and persistent vein of ore, usually gold.

BULLION. A term used to describe raw gold that is ready to be shipped to the mint. When the metal has been reduced to nearly pure form, it is then cast into bars or ingots for easy storage and shipping. Occasionally other forms were used. The famous Bullion Mine in the Cariboo once melted one big clean-up into the form of a large naval gun-shell. It weighed 4,745 ounces and was valued at $81,622.

BYPRODUCT. A secondary product obtained when mining something else. For example,

John Likely, John Hobson and an unidentified guard beside gold bullion from the Cariboo Hydraulic mine near Likely, B.C.

gold is often a byproduct of a copper mining operation, which means copper is the main metal mined, but some gold is also recovered.

CACHE. This was a temporary hiding place for gold or other wealth, including supplies, food or equipment. Basically, anything hidden by the owner until his return.

CALAVERITE. A telluride of gold and silver, usually granular in structure, with a silver-white metallic lustre: an important ore of gold.

CARAT. A measure of weight for gold or precious gems. Pure gold is 24 carats.

CELESTIAL. An expression used to describe Chinese miners. The term was in wide-spread use during the California gold rush, and was brought to British Columbia when the Forty-Niners came north. The word originated from the Celestial Empire of China.

CEMENTED GRAVEL. A hard, tightly-packed material that is frequently rich in gold.

CHAMOIS. A kind of soft leather used to squeeze out the mercury from the amalgam before burning.

CHINA DIGGINGS. A term used to describe an area which was abandoned by whites as unprofitable, but was still being worked by the Chinese. Some of them often proved to be far richer than the white man thought.

CHINA WAGES. A term used to describe the wages accepted by Chinese workers which was considered low or unacceptable to white miners.

CLAIM. An area that has been filed with the proper government agency for the extraction of gold or other metals. It gave the prospector the rights to the minerals within his claim for a certain period of time. The boundaries of the claim were to be marked by stakes, piles of rock, etc. A can containing the description and particulars of the claim was usually placed on or near one of the posts.

CLAIM JUMPER. Someone who seizes, or illegally re-stakes a claim which has already been filed by another prospector.

CLAY. See **Cemented Gravel.**

CLEAN-UP. A term used to describe the cleaning-up of concentrates from the riffles of rockers, sluices, dredges, etc., after the gold-bearing gravel has been washed. These concentrates are then processed, usually through amalgamation, to recover the gold.

COARSE GOLD. Rough, unrefined nuggets of gold which vary in size. Gold that has travelled a considerable distance is usually worn smooth; therefore, coarse gold is an indication of limited travel.

COLOUR. A term used to describe the minute specs of gold in gravel. Colours, though themselves minuscule, are indicators of gold in a particular stream or river.

CONCENTRATES. This is the name given to the material that remains in the gold pan, rocker, sluice, etc., after washing. Concentrates are usually composed of black sands, gold and silver, but particles of platinum and a variety of other minerals could be included.

CONDUIT. A channel or pipe used for conveying water.

CORE DRILL. These are usually core samples extracted from solid rock to test for mineral content without blasting away tons of rock.

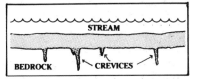

CREVICE. A crack or narrow fissure in bedrock which tends to accumulate and trap gold. Small cracks can hold large quantities of gold, and are usually the best prospect for the gold panner.

DEAD WORK. This phrase was used by prospectors to describe the work of clearing away overburden to get at the gold-bearing gravel.

DEPOSITS. This usually refers to an area where gold or other metal has been found. There are two types of placer deposits; eluvial deposits, located near the originating lode; and alluvial deposits, found at considerable distances from the originating lode.

Gold dredges like this have played an important role in taking a quarter billion dollars in gold from the Klondike area. This scene is on Bonanza Creek, Yukon, close to Carmack's Discovery Claim.

DIGGINGS. This name usually applied to claims that were currently being worked for gold, silver, or other ore.

DISCOVERY CLAIM. This was the first claim filed on a given stream or river. The other claims were then staked above or below the discovery claim, which was legally larger than any other claim on the creek.

DREDGE. A dredge is a machine used for scooping or sucking the gold-bearing gravel from the river bed. There are numerous types and sizes, ranging from the small portable compact models that can easily be transported by one man, to large barge-type dredges for clearing mud from harbour entrances. Next to hydraulic mining, nothing destroys the landscape faster than dredges.

DRIFT. "Drift" mining simply means tunnelling a horizontal shaft that leads from a central deposit of ore. Drifts can run for hundreds, even thousands of feet, as miners traced tiny seams of gold fanning out from the original strike.

A dog hauling ore from a drift in the Klondike.

DRY PLACER. A deposit of gold or precious metal found on dry ground.

DRY WASHER. This is a device used to work claims without the use of water. Instead, a small billows blows away the light materials, leaving gold and heavy particles to be panned later.

A modern dry washer at work.

DUCTILITY. The ability of metals to be drawn out in fine wires without breaking.

DUST. This term refers to particles of gold so minute that they resemble dust. In the old days, the amount of gold dust a miner could pinch between his thumb and forefinger constituted $1, while a whisky glass full was worth $100.

ELDORADO. Originally derived from the Spanish, referring to a legend about a land of gold and plenty. It is now used frequently to describe a place of fabulous wealth, a region abounding in gold and precious gems.

ELECTRUM. An alloy of gold and silver.

FELDSPAR. A constituent of granite, basalt, and other igneous rocks, that form a large part of the earth's crust. Clay is the chief substance formed when weathering decomposes feldspars. (See also **Bedrock.**)

FINE GOLD. Generally, this term re-

fers to gold which can pass through a 40-mesh screen. It includes fine gold and dust, which in your pan, will appear as colours so small that it can only be collected by amalgamation.

FINENESS. This is a word used to indicate the purity of gold.

FLAKE GOLD. These are small chips of gold, or pieces that have been flattened in transit.

FLAT. A word describing a level spot, often near a stream or river, that was suitable for a settlement.

FLOTATION PROCESS. A method for recovering gold from crushed ore and concentrates.

FLOUR GOLD. An extremely fine gold that is difficult to save. It is uneconomical to pan flour gold because of its almost powdery size and weight.

FOOL'S GOLD. (See **Pyrite.**)

FLUME. An inclined waterway, most often a channel dug in the hillside to

A sluice at work on Bonanza Creek in the Yukon.

transport water to hydraulic mining camps. Simply described, they are similar to a long series of sluices, and in fact, the name flume was once synonymous with sluice.

FRACTION. A small portion of ground lying between two claims which could not be staked by either as it exceeded their legal limits. "Twelve-foot" Davis was so-named after a 12-foot fraction on Williams Creek which he worked between two other claims. After recovering about $12,000, Davis sold the fraction, which then yielded over $100,000.

FREE MINER. Anyone over 18 years of age who possesses a Free Miner's Certificate, which entitles the holder to prospect legally and to stake claims.

FULMINATE OF MERCURY. An explosive substance made by dissolving mercury in nitric acid and adding alcohol.

GANGUE. The worthless materials associated with metal ore deposits.

GEOLOGY. The science of the rocks and strata of the earth's crust.

GIANT MONITOR. An apparatus fitted with a nozzle used in hydraulic

Hydraulicking on Bonanza Creek. Originally the miners worked their claims by digging down to bedrock and washing the recovered gravels. Hydraulicking was considerably easier, but relied upon a ready water supply.

A prospector washing gravel with a "grizzly" near Edmonton in 1890.

mining. Water is forced through the nozzle under great pressure, then directed against gold-bearing gravel. The material is then washed into sluices where the gold can be separated.

GLORY HOLE. A term used by miners to describe a small, but usually rich deposit of gold.

GOLDBEATER. Someone who beats gold into thin sheets.

GOLD LEAF. Gold beaten into extremely thin sheets.

GOLD RUSH. The wild scramble by prospectors to reach the new goldfields. (See Chapter 1.)

GRADIENT. The slope or descent of a stream or river.

GRAIN. This term is used to describe small particles of gold, and is also used as a unit of weight. (See **Avoirdupois** and **Troy Weights.**)

GRAVEL. The gold-bearing material in a stream which you must wash to recover gold.

GRIZZLY. A device used to keep rocks and boulders out of a sluice box.

HALF-LIFE. The rate of decay of radioactive materials.

HALOGENS. Any member of the family of very active elements consisting of fluorine, chlorine, bromine, and iodine. Chemically, the halogens re-

Hardrock mining at Bralorne, B.C. in 1938.

semble one another closely and form a saline compound by simple combination with a metal.

HARDROCK MINING. This usually refers to quartz mining and is said to have originated in California about 1850. First a main shaft had to be sunk, then horizontal shafts or drifts would be cut that followed the various seams of gold as it led from the main deposit. As this type of mining required a sizeable investment, the small operator was quickly eliminated.

HEAD FRAME. This applied to the heavy timber frame found above most hardrock mine sites. It was used to hoist ore from the depths of the mine, and also an elevator to hoist and lower workmen.

HEMATITE. A form of native iron ore, blood-red in colour.

HIDDEN VALUE. The unseen values usually found in black sands, which in many cases could not be detected by the naked eye.

HOPPER. The tray in the upper end of a rocker.

HYDRAULIC MINING. In hydraulic mining, water under great pressure was discharged through monitors against a gold-bearing hillside. The force of the water would wash away the hillside, flushing the silt and gravel through sluices where it could be separated and the gold recovered. Hydraulicking could — and often did — completely ruin the landscape.

HYDROCHLORIC ACID. The only known compound of hydrogen and chlorine made by dissolving the corrosive gaseous compound, hydrogen chlorine, in water. (See also **Aqua Regia**.)

Weight 4745½ Oz Value $81,622.00

To Bank of Montreal.
MONTREAL.
CANADA.
From Cariboo Hydraulic Mining Co.

Quesnelle Forks B.C.

(Above) Shaped like a naval gun shell, this block of gold from the famous Bullion Pit, near Likely, weighed 4745½ ounces and was valued in 1900s at $81,622. Today, it would be worth $2,135,250.
(Below) A Long Tom in action. One man is bailing water while the other shovels gravel. Coarse coco-matting covers the bottom of the sluice box.

INGOT. A metal bar, especially or silver or gold, usually cast from a mould for convenience in handling and measuring.

IRIDIUM. A brittle, silver-grey, metallic element of extreme hardness belonging to the platinum group. Discovered by William Tennant in 1904, it is used in certain alloys, for pen-points, jewellery, etc.

JADE. A very hard, semi-precious stone, usually dark green in colour, that is carved for ornaments or used in jewellery. Frequently found in British Columbia.

JIG. A partly or fully-submerged screen that is shaken to wash or sort particles by weight and size. Also called a Jigger.

LODE. A metallic vein in the earth's crust, especially silver or gold. These lodes were the original source of placer gold.

LONG TOM. This was a special sluice

box of extra length so that it could capture extra fine particles of gold. Some times known as the Long Tom Sluice.

LOW GRADE. Deposits of gold, silver, or other metals, which exist in insufficient quantities to be worked economically, except through large scale methods.

MAGNETITE. A magnetic form of iron also known as lodestone. (See **Black Sand.**)

MALLEABLE. The ability of a metal to be hammered without breaking.

MARCASITE. A white iron pyrite used in jewellery because of its brilliance.

MERCURY. A heavy, liquid metal, silvery-white in colour, with a very low melting point. Used to recover gold, silver and platinum from concentrates. Also called Quicksilver.

METALLURGY. The art of working metals or of obtaining metals from ores.

MONITOR. (See **Giant Monitor.**)

MOSS. Small, thickly growing, cryptogamous plant which thrives on moist surfaces. Gold often accumulates in moss, which should be broken up and panned carefully before discarding.

MOTHER LODE. A vein or streak of gold or other precious metal in the earth's crust from which placer deposits originate.

NITRIC ACID. A highly corrosive, colourless liquid that emits choking fumes into the air. A diluted solution is used to clean the gold-bearing concentrates before amalgamation, and also to clean mercury that has become dirty. (See also **Aqua Regia.**)

NOBLE METALS. Metals which do

This nugget, weighing 73 ounces, was found on McDame Creek in 1877 by Alfred Freeman. It is the biggest gold nugget ever found in B.C.

Mel Clark, of Fort St. John, B.C., demonstrates the gold panning skill that made him the World's Class A Gold Panning Champion in 1972.

not have great chemical activity, particularly gold, which is neither corroded by moisture nor affected by oxygen or ordinary acids.

NOVICE. An amateur or inexperienced prospector or miner.

NUGGET. A rough lump or mass of native gold of no particular size. These range in size from the head of a match to nearly 200 pounds. The largest United States nugget, weighing 195 pounds, came from California. The largest in British Columbia, weighing 73 ounces, came from McDame Creek.

OIL. The preservative coating which must be burned off steel gold pans before using.

OLD CHANNEL. (See **Ancient Stream Bed.**)

ORE. Rock containing metals or their compounds in sufficient quantities to be mined.

OUNCE A DAY. In the early days, ground that yielded an ounce of gold a day, through panning, was considered rich ground.

OUTCROP. The point where the vein or lode of a metal comes to the surface of the earth's crust and is visible.

OVERBURDEN. Generally, the low grade material which must be cleared away to get at the rich gold-bearing gravel just above bedrock.

PALLADIUM. A rare metallic element occurring in combination with platinum, iridium, and rhodium. It is silver-white, malleable, ductile and does not tarnish in the air.

PAN. A broad shallow vessel of metal or plastic used to wash gold-bearing gravel.

PANNING. The art of washing gold-bearing gravel with a gold pan, batea or other similar vessel.

PAY. A word used to describe gold-bearing gravel that returns wages or better to the miner.

PAY DIRT. This term is used to describe an area where a prospector has found gold; e.g. "struck pay dirt."

PENNYWEIGHT. A Troy weight of 24 grains. (See **Troy Weights.**)

PETER OUT. A common expression that applied to a claim, mine, or deposit that had been thoroughly worked over, leaving only the worthless rubble behind.

PLACER. Generally, this word refers to deposits of gold-bearing gravel. (See **Deposits.**)

PLACER MINING. The act of recovering gold from placer deposits by means of a gold pan, rocker, sluice, dredge, etc. Placer mining depends largely on water for washing and separating the gold and gravel. (See Chapter 6.)

PLATINUM. A rare, whitish, steel-grey malleable metal. It is harder than gold, but very ductile. It is very infusible and resistant to most acids, has a high electrical resistance, and is widely used as a catalyst, for jewellery, and in dental work. Usually found native, but also in combination with gold. In B.C. it was discovered in the Similkameen region with gold, but was initially discarded as worth-

The Rocker

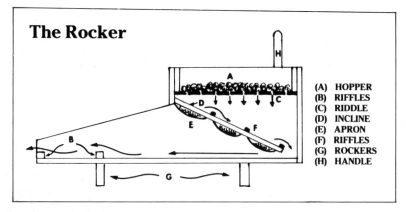

(A) HOPPER
(B) RIFFLES
(C) RIDDLE
(D) INCLINE
(E) APRON
(F) RIFFLES
(G) ROCKERS
(H) HANDLE

less by all except the Chinese.

PLAYED-OUT. (See **Peter Out.**)

POCKET. An unusually large concentration of gold in a small area was often referred to as a "pocket." (See also **Glory Hole.**)

POKE. A small leather bag or pouch, usually two inches wide by six inches deep, with a drawstring at the top. These were used as wallets by miners to carry gold dust and nuggets.

POORMAN'S DIGGINGS. This term did not mean that the area being worked was low grade or yielding small quantities of gold; rather that it could be worked by a miner with a rocker or sluice with little capital. Hence, it could be worked by a poor man.

POT HOLE. A cavity formed in bedrock by the action of stones in the eddy of a stream. They are highly overrated as gold producers, as the gold is eventually ground into fine dust and escapes.

PRODUCTION. The total yield or "production" of gold or other precious metal from a mine, claim or deposit.

PROSPECTING. The act of searching for gold, silver, copper, lead, or any other valuable metal. In the case of placer gold deposits, the prospector retrieves the gold as he finds it, thus becoming a miner. If lodes or low grade metals are located, the prospector usually sells or leases the rights to them to a large mining company which has the necessary equipment and resources to mine them, and he continues looking, or "prospecting" for new finds.

PUDDLING BOX. A box used to break up tough clay or cemented gravel.

PYRITE. A name for many compounds of metal with sulphur or arsenic, especially iron pyrites or copper pyrites. Pyrite is brass-yellow and brittle, but because of its colour, it is often mistaken for gold; hence the name "fool's gold."

QUARTZ. One of the most common materials found in the mother lode. It consists of pure silica or silicon dioxide and is formed in massive and in hexagonal crystals. Quartz may be transparent, translucent, opaque,

A string of rockers in action at King Solomon's Hill, Yukon, in 1898.

colourless or coloured. Most of the hardrock mining done for gold comes from quartz veins.

QUICKSILVER. (See **Mercury.**)

REAGENT. Any substance, generally in solution, employed to bring about a characteristic reaction in a chemical analysis.

RECOVERY. The act of "recovering" fine gold from the heavy concentrates, usually through amalgamation. (See Chapter 5.)

REFINE. To reduce crude metals to a finer, purer state.

RETORT. An apparatus used to separate an amalgam of gold and mercury, through heating, which saves the mercury for future use.

RHODIUM. A hard, silver-white metallic element found in river sands or rocks associated with other members of the platinum family to which it belongs.

RICH. Ground where gold or other precious metals abound.

RIDDLE. A large perforated iron sheet which forms the bottom of the hopper in a rocker, used in screening or sifting gravel.

RIFFLES. Simply stated, these are obstructions which line the bottom of a rocker, sluice or dredge, collecting the fine gold. Different types of riffles include: common riffles, zigzag riffles, block riffles, stone riffles, pole riffles, etc.

RIM. The outer border or edge of a

gold pan.

ROCKER. A device consisting of a box which rests on "rockers," and which is used to wash placer deposits.

SKIM. The practice of removing froth from the surface during the floatation method of recovering gold.

SLOPE. The gradient of a stream or terrain.

SLUICE BOX. The sluice box was invented by a party of Nevada miners in 1850. It consisted of a large trough leading down from their claim to their Long Tom. The sluice was an immediate success, becoming a stan-

A sluice box, showing canvas covered by coarse expanded metal screen riffles, with bar riffles below.

dard tool of the California gold rush, and was later brought north into Canada.

SLUICING. The act of washing gold from river gravels through the use of a sluice box.

SNIPING. In miner's jargon, this word meant the act of prospecting and re-working old claims, dumps, and other sites that have been abandoned. It also refers to cleaning out bedrock cracks.

STAKE. This could refer to the act of "staking" a legal claim by following the necessary regulations (see **Claim**), or it could refer to the occasions when a miner had accumulated enough gold to retire, either temporarily or permanently. In the latter case, the miner is said to have "made a stake."

STAMP MILL. A piece of heavy machinery that is power-operated and smashes the hardrock ore into a powder so that it can be processed for gold or other precious metal.

STRIKE. This usually denoted the discovery of gold or silver. Once a "strike," or discovery had been made, hundreds, or even thousands, of gold seekers would swarm into the area.

SUCTION DREDGE. (See **Dredge.**)

TAILINGS. This word describes the waste material that is left or discarded after the gold is removed. Also called dumps, these are generally piles of rocks or debris left from the mining operation. Once considered worthless, tailings have become a target for modern prospectors. Occasionally large nuggets were discarded

Cleaning bedrock by hand after hydraulic operations on Germansen Creek, B.C. The man is picking a small piece of gold with tweezers. Note the whisk and spoon to the left.

with the stones; or valuable metals, unknown to early prospectors, were tossed aside.

TAILING WHEELS. These were wheels used to transport the waste material from the mines to a place some distance away.

TRANSMUTATION. (See **Alchemy.**)

TRAY. (See **Hopper.**)

TRESTLE. In mining, a trestle is a wooden frame consisting of braced legs fixed underneath horizontal bars, used to support a sluice or series of sluices.

TRIBUTARY. A branch of a stream flowing into a larger stream.

TROUGH. A long, open vessel carrying water and gold-bearing gravel.

TORY WEIGHT. A system of weight measurement for precious gems and metals. This system is different from avoirdupois weight with which most of us are familiar.

24 grains . . . . 1 pennyweight
20 pennyweights . . . . . 1 troy ounce
12 troy ounces . . . . . 1 troy pound

UNALLOYED. A metal in the pure state, unalloyed with any other metal.

UNDERCURRENT. A current under the surface of the main stream, sometimes flowing in a contrary direction.

UNPRODUCTIVE. A mine or stream that was abandoned because it was unprofitable to work. Due to the recent escalation in the price of gold, many of these abandoned areas are being reopened.

WASTE. Any material that is consi-

dered worthless after the gold has been removed. (See **Tailings.**)

WEATHERED. A term meaning well-worn, generally referring to bedrock, and a result of glacial and water action.

WET PLACER. A deposit of gold or other precious metal located under water.

WHEEL. This refers to a variety of water-wheels employed to provide water for mining.

WING-DAM. This was a dam that divided a stream bed miners wanted to work, lengthwise, allowing water to flow through sluice boxes and other devices set up to wash the gravel. These were put to effective use on the Fraser River.

WORKED OUT. (See **Peter Out.**)

The Davis Wheel and flume at Williams Creek.

BIBLIOGRAPHY

Barlee, N.L. *The Guide to Gold Panning.*

Downs, Art. *Wagon Road North,* Foremost Publishing, 1973.

Hogan, J.J. *Gold,* Mines & Resources, 1972.

Keene, Jerry. "The Gold Pan," *Treasure* magazine.

Keene, Jerry. "Gold in a Campground."

Lang, A.H. *Prospecting in Canada,* Canada Geological Society, 1969.

Legaye, E.S. *Gold: The ABC's of Panning,* Western Heritage press, 1970.

Lewis, Jack. *Treasure Hunter's Digest,"* Digest Books, inc., 1975.

Matthews, Down. "Gold: Boom or Bunkum?" *True Treasure* magazine, 1967.

McClelland, K. "Gold Throughout The Ages," *True Treasure* magazine, 1968.

McClelland, K. "Solid Gold Facts," *True Treasure* magazine, 1969.

Stevens, Lucky. "How To Use a Mercury Retort," *Western Treasure* magazine, 1972.

The Columbia Encyclopedia, Columbia University Press, 1969.

Dictionary of Science, Dell, 1919.

Guinness Book of World Records, Norris & Ross McWhirter, 1970.

Merit School Encyclopedia, Macmillan Educational Corp., 1973.

"How to Get Started Finding Gold," *Western Treasure Annual,* 1970.

"Recovering Fine Gold," *Treasure* magazine.

B.C. Minister of Mines Reports, various issues.